HIP-HOP RHYMING DICTIONARY

IR RAPPERS,
JS AND MCs

..dVIN M. MITCHELL

Published by Firebrand Music
Los Angeles

Distributed by Alfred

Library of Congress Control Number: 2003107925

The author is grateful to Lauren Mitchell for everything and
then some; Mike Rutledge and Susan Christiansen for their
wise advice; the amazing, talented people at Firebrand, including
Ted Engelbart, Link Harnsberger, Kim Kasabian and most of all
Ed Lyon, who was the catalyst for the project to begin with.

Table of Contents

Introduction

Alonzo Westbrook writes in his *Hip Hoptionary*:

> Rap is like a slave song speaking of the
> conditions and hopes of a people spinning
> words and communicating ideas in codes;
> hiding behind a language only to reveal its
> absolute strength and metaphorical depths.

The *Hip-Hop Rhyming Dictionary* was put together in the hope that it will help the rapper, the hip-hop artist, the DJ, and the MC in their creative process and hopefully contribute to their quest to "reveal the absolute strength" of the art.

Most words are cross-referenced in more than one place to make it easy to find just the right word. Only the most frequently used words of the contemporary artist are listed here. Every editorial or formatting decision was made based on this image: It's late, you're sitting with pen in hand, and you've got the beat pulsating in your head—but you need the *right* rhymes. You grab this book, look up a word, and find many choices, one of which is *the* one—the only one—that truly expresses what you want to say.

Also, use this book as a source of inspiration. Spend time flipping through it. Discover great words you've never thought of before, and let the book help you express yourself in bold, new ways.

Finally, keep me posted on what works, what doesn't, what's missing, and what's new and should be added in the next edition at HipHopRhymingBook@yahoo.com. Would love to hear the success stories, too.

Peace.

Kevin M. Mitchell

How This Book Works

Traditional rhyming books take many pages to explain how to use them—and even then, it's still hard to find your way around. This book is for the hip-hop artist who wants to spend his or her time *writing*, not reading. It's so easy you don't even have to read this section, but for those who gotta know the method behind the madness, here it is.

Format

Formatting this dictionary was not without its challenges. Words are cross-referenced: If you want to rhyme *bad,* look up *bad,* and you'll find *sad.* If you want to rhyme *sad,* look up *sad,* and you'll find *bad,* etc. But there are over 400 words that rhyme with *be.* To cross-reference them as previously described would create a volume roughly the size and weight of a Humvee.

In such instances, a "key word" was chosen (in this example, *be*) and all the possible words rhyming with that are listed under the key word. So when you look up *fantasy,* you find this:

fantasy (see **be**)

That means that there are too many rhymes to list under all entries, and *be* is the key word. Then, simply look up *be,* and you'll find *fantasy,* along with a few hundred other common rhymes.

In the few instances where there are more than 100 rhymes for an entry, the words are grouped by the number of syllables (one syllable, two syllables, etc.).

Remember, the key word is often the most common, simplest word. So if you're trying to rhyme *mitigate* and it's not listed, look up a simpler word that rhymes with it (like *hate*). There you'll find all the words you need to rhyme with *mitigate.* This situation is rare indeed, but it's helpful to keep in mind if you're trying to rhyme a large word containing many syllables.

Broken Rules

Other rhyming dictionaries are too clumsy for the contemporary rapper—or any songwriter for that matter. They have rigid rules of what rhymes, not taking into account different pronunciations or ways you can enunciate words to make them rhyme. For example, under *flattery* is only the word *battery*. But hip-hop artists have been creative about redefining what rhymes and what doesn't—so creative, that capturing all the possibilities is impossible. But a few alternatives have been attempted here, for example:

flattery battery (see *be*)

This means that *battery* is all that rhymes with *flattery*, but if you look up *be* (indicated by italics), you'll find other words that can work in a song. This cross-reference is also used when, depending on your dialect or accent, some other words are available that could possibly rhyme if pronounced in a certain way.

So when the word following "see" is in bold:

among (see **young**)

it means that the word is offered as a "strict" rhyme; when the referenced word is in italics, it is a suggestion of other possible rhymes.

Listen to any great song—East Coast, West Coast, old school—and you'll find a wealth of clever rhymes. This book doesn't try to do that, but leaves the bending of syllables and the way things are pronounced and emphasized to your creative selves.

Slang words and colloquialisms are included whenever possible and appropriate. Under the word *anchor,* for example, you'll find *thank 'er.*

Names, Places, Expressions, Clichés

Names (*José*), famous people (*Nelly*), and places (*Trinidad*) are often included. These tend to be included when there are fewer rhymes in general; I was less likely to list them for words with many rhymes. Common, everyday expressions and short clichés are also included wherever possible—and hopefully those listed will get you thinking of others that might be found in your corner of the world but aren't included here.

Prefixes and Suffixes

You can create more words by adding prefixes and suffixes. At the top of every dictionary page is a running header listing some of the most common prefixes and suffixes. When you're looking at a word, look up at the header and mix and match what's there with the word you're looking at to create other words.

The more likely it is that a word could appear in a song, the more likely it's included in the initial list. (For example, under *view*, you'll find *review* and *preview*, etc.)

If you are trying to rhyme a word that has a prefix or suffix already built in and you don't find it, don't give up. You should find it in its original form. For example, if you're looking up *viewing*, and you don't find it, simply take off the suffix (in this case, *-ing*), and look up *view*. There you'll find a list of words that only need the *-ing* added to find the rhyme that's right for you.

Words Left Out

In addition to words that would probably never be used in a rap, a few common words were left out that had only one or two rhymes.

Words found offensive are also left out because there are only so many trees we can slay to make this book, and these words are too obvious (besides, I think we got all those down). The point of this book is to make the most room for the more original, less prevalent, choices.

The Art of Rap Writing

Rapping is a craft, not just talent and attitude. Since you have the heart and will to express yourself, working at the craft is the only way you'll get where you want to be.

You'll only become a crowd mover by doing a lot of writing and by pushing yourself to new limits. When 50 Cent was shipped to upstate New York by Columbia Records, he turned out 36 songs in 2 1/2 weeks. Later, after being shot and then unceremoniously dropped from Columbia, he cranked out another 30 songs in a short period of time to create the buzz that would get him signed to Eminem's label. That's not atypical. Tupac, too, was notorious for his fanatical devotion to work, wearing out all those around him who tried to keep up. Dig into the history of your favorite artist and it's likely you'll find a workaholic. On the other hand, Vanilla Ice is imagined to have watched a lot of the tube. You catch the drift.

So never be satisfied with something that's not your best. Always be working on improving a piece of music; then quickly move on and write another. Here's my theory: All writers have 100 bad songs in them that they have to work out of their system before they start writing words that are any good. Part of the reason for this is that so many songs by others have seeped into our pores that we're simply regurgitating what we've heard on the radio and from our CD collection. That's why it's important to write a lot. It's the only way you'll get your feet wet.

Five Tips to Better Writing

1. Save everything. Don't throw away anything you write. Keep your lyrics in a box, a folder, a file, wherever—save them even if you immediately dislike them. Later, when you're having a bout of writer's block or just want other ideas, looking through the proverbial junkyard of songs-gone-wrong can be helpful. Even if most of the lyrics are bad, later you may look back and spot one line that was really good—and then want to lift it for your new song.

2. Analyze others. Few things in our artistic life happen by accident. Good writing usually doesn't happen spontaneously—at least not all the time. Words are formed, molded, shaped, and worked for maximum effect. Take a favorite rap that moves you. Is it telling a story? Relaying a feeling? How does it do that? Specifically, what line or lines? The hook? What about it makes you think of something that has happened in your own life? Are there unexpected rhymes and words that come out of nowhere? Study the work of the masters. Live, listen, and learn.

3. Analyze yourself. Develop the ability to look at your work objectively. Often people think that everything they do stinks—or that everything they do is great. Chances are, the truth is somewhere in between. Be able to separate yourself from the story or feeling you were trying to convey, and ask yourself: Is this working? What am I trying to say? Learn to distinguish between the good, the bad, and the ugly in your work.

4. Cool off. When you write a rap, you'll probably love it right away. But put it away for a few days—if not a week. Later, with an objective eye, you will be in a better position to fine tune the rap and spot the tune's weaknesses. Don't hesitate to hack at your lyrics, and also have the courage to cut a good line if it's not right for the song.

5. Avoid clichés. After you've written your song and have given yourself a suitable cooling-off period, sit down and go over it for what are called the "land mines of bad lyric writing"—clichés. Look at every line, and every rhyme: Have you heard it before? A *million* times before? Is there a better choice out there?

Keep doin' what you're doin'. And keep the faith.

A Brief History: "Rap Was Always Here"

Rap always has been here in history. They say when God talked to the prophets, he was rappin' to them. You could go and pick up the old Shirley Ellis records, "The Name Game." "The Clapping Song," Moms Mabley, Pigmeat Markham, when he made "Here Comes the Judge." You could pick up Barry White with his love type of rap, or Isaac Hayes. You could get your militancy message rap coming from Malcolm X, Minster Louis Farrakhan, Muhammad Ali. A lot of time, the Black people used to play this game called The Dozens on each other, rappin' about your mama or your father and stuff. So rap was always here.

—Afrika Bambaataa

Yes, Yes, Y'all: Oral History of Hip-Hop's First Decade
Jim Fricke, Charlie Ahearn

While rhyming has been around since the beginning of time, rap's roots are found in African oral tradition, where the sparring with words was always a part of the culture.

But hip-hop clearly started on the New York City streets, specifically the Bronx, in the early 1970s. In 1973, when unemployment was high, crime and drugs were rampant, police corruption commonplace, and as the city slid into bankruptcy, a Jamaican DJ named **Kool Herc** started improvising rhymes over the instrumental sections of his obscure albums at parties. To extend his time on the mic, he added a second duplicate album and an audio mixer; he was the first one to do this, and was the first to treat the turntable as a musical instrument. He and his imitators did it everywhere—you could hear strains of this new sound at block parties, community centers, clubs, and even parks.

Soon others followed, including **Afrika Bambaataa**, who introduced sampling and synthesizers. He assumed the title "Godfather of Rap," and would eventually cross over to work with such diverse artists as the Sex Pistols' John Lydon, Sly & Robbie, UB40, and Boy George. Then there was **Grandmaster Flash**. Flash spent his teen years DJing at parties and in parks in the Bronx, and after years of experimentation, developed the scratch-mixing technique. To this new sound he added a few friends who would rap over the mix. This group eventually became known as Grandmaster Flash and the Furious Five.

"The teenagers of the South Bronx and Harlem didn't have the money to pay for admission to the expensive midtown and downtown clubs, so they had their own parties," writes **Kurtis Blow**, an early MC and DJ on the scene. "Along the way, clubs, house parties, and block parties sprang up all over New York ghettos, giving birth to the neighborhood DJ and MC. Something of a mutation of disco, hip-hop was also a rebellion against disco." (Blow would go on to release "The Breaks," which was the first certified-gold rap record, in 1980. He would also be the first rap artist to sign with a major label and the first rapper to appear on a national TV show, *Soul Train*.)

But it was the **Sugar Hill Gang** that broke out of the parks and parties and onto the national charts. Their "Rapper's Delight" hinted at the mass-market potential of the new music, but while it hit number 36 on the Billboard charts, those on the scene felt that the group's songs were inferior to the level of work other groups were producing. Yet it did open the floodgates to other rappers.

Pop and rock musicians (including new-wave rockers **Blondie**, who incorporated rap into their hit song "Rapture" in 1980), particularly white ones, began to embrace the new style of these black groups, and despite the naysayers it was clear that rap was no mere fad. The year 1985 proved to be a pivotal one. **LL Cool J**'s first single, "I Can't Live Without My Radio," released when he was just 17, showed what was to come. His hard-hitting and street-wise music featured spare beats and complex rhythms. The next year, his ballad "I Need Love" became one of the first pop-rap crossover hits.

One of the most influential artists was **Run-DMC**, who considered themselves a rock-rap band because their songs were three to four minutes long and had a chorus, structurally similar to rock. They focused on the music, rejecting the 1970s rappers' flamboyant stage costumes and adopting the baggy clothing style instead. In 1986, they joined with Aerosmith on the hit song "Walk This Way," which received heavy rotation on MTV. (This also gave the aging rock group a much-needed shot in the arm.)

Also in 1986, rap reached the top 10 on the Billboard pop charts. Controversially, the milestone wasn't reached by a DJ with true inner-city street credentials, but by three white kids from privileged suburban New York families. The party anthem "(You Gotta) Fight for Your Right (To Party!)" by the **Beastie Boys** blended hard rock and rap. They went on tour opening for Madonna, and were nightly booed off the stage. Later, they fared better opening for Run-DMC, but their success brought criticism. Rap fans called them cultural pirates while others charged that the band's lyrics were sexist and violent.

The first female rap group of consequence, **Salt-N-Pepa**, released the single "Push It" (1987), which reached the top 20 on Billboard's pop charts. In the late 1980s, a large segment of rap became highly politicized, resulting in the most overt social agenda in popular music since the urban folk movement of the 1960s. The groups **Public Enemy** and **Boogie Down Productions** epitomized this political style of rap. Public Enemy came to prominence in 1988 with their second album *It Takes a Nation of Millions to Hold Us Back,* and their song "Fight the Power" was featured in Spike Lee's masterpiece *Do the Right Thing*.

In 1988, the first major album of gangsta rap was released: *Straight Outta Compton* by the West-Coast rap group **N.W.A**. This was one of the first hip-hop groups to see its members go on to successful solo careers—**Dr. Dre**, **Ice Cube**, and **MC Ren** all released albums that went platinum and multi-platinum. With a strong beat that occasionally referred to 1970s funk, the band's music was always second to their message.

Queen Latifah released *All Hail the Queen* in 1989, and many critics and fans felt her feminist perspective was a welcome respite from the increasingly violent and misogynistic raps of her male contemporaries. Taking it to the opposite extreme was **Lil' Kim**'s release of *Hardcore* in 1996, where she rapped about sex and Uzis and proved in her powerhouse debut that she was hungry and bold, and that her work was a match to whatever her male counterparts could dish out.

In 1992, **Ice Cube**'s *The Predator* was the first album to receive a debut on both the pop and R&B charts at number one. Also debuting that year was an underground track, "Protect Ya Neck," by **Wu-Tang Clan**. This nine-member rap group, headed and produced by **RZA**, emerged to find their way onto radio stations, and their unique Afro-Asiatic discipline in the art of rhyming made them radically popular and influential.

As the 1990s evolved, rap did too. It became increasingly eclectic and was both influential and itself influenced by everything from jazz to heavy metal to punk. As rap became increasingly part of the American mainstream in the 1990s, political rap became less prominent while gangsta rap, as epitomized by the **Geto Boys**, **Snoop Doggy Dogg**, and **Tupac Shakur**, grew in popularity. At the other end of this explicit and violent trend were **MC Hammer**, **Will Smith**, and **Vanilla Ice**, who emphasized the pop, overly commercialized side of rap.

In 1994, **Notorious B.I.G.**'s debut album *Ready to Die* made him one of the most popular hip-hop performers of the mid-1990s. He used his deep voice and potent lyrics about urban street life to prove that he was going to be a major player on the scene. Tragically, his debut title would prove a prophecy, and like too many rising stars his career ended prematurely with his murder in 1997.

Eminem was nine when he heard **Ice-T**'s *Reckless* and became caught up on gangsta/hip-hop sounds. He spent his youth hustling demo tapes and earning local infamy as one half of the Detroit duo Soul Intent. He released his solo independent debut album *Infinite* in 1996 and quickly caught the attention of Dr. Dre, who became his mentor. He would go on to dominate the Grammys and charts.

50 Cent had just signed with Columbia Records when, in April of 2000, he was shot nine times. During his recovery, Columbia Records dropped him from his contract. After consulting with Dr. Dre, he signed up with Eminem's label, reportedly for over a million dollars. His 2003 release *Get Rich or Die Tryin'* went straight to number one and sold 1.5 million copies in its first week and a half.

Hip-hop is now pervasive everywhere, as a culture and as a music, and rapping is heard regularly in alternative rock acts just as new hip-hop stars are created every year. Like blues, rock, and other predecessors, hip-hop will continue to evolve and reach new levels—both highs and lows. It'll mature as it combines more elements from jazz, rock, pop, and blues in addition to inevitably rediscovering its old school roots.

But at the heart, it'll always be some kid in a Bronx park with a pair of turntables and a microphone.

> "I think Hip-Hop is diverse. It's gotten to a state now that doesn't really have any color in music, it's jazz, rock and roll, R&B. So I think that's the level that hip-hop is going to, and I think it will keep branching out."

-Pepa, of Salt-N-Pepa

Recommended Reading

Fight the Power: Rap, Race, and Reality.
 By Chuck D., Yusuf Jah (contributor). Published by
 Delta Press. 1998.

Hip-Hop America.
 By Nelson George. Published by Penguin Books. 1999.

Hip Hoptionary: The Dictionary of Hip-Hop Terminology.
 By Alonzo Westbrook. Published by Harlem Moon, a division of
 Random House. 2002.

Turntable Technique: The Art of the DJ.
 By Stephen Webber. Published by Berklee Press and distributed
 by Numark. 2001.

Vibe Hip-Hop Divas.
 By Vibe Magazine editors and writers. Published by Three Rivers
 Press. 2001.

Vibe History of Hip Hop.
 By Alan Light (editor). Published by Three Rivers Press. 1999.

Yes, Yes, Y'all: Oral History of Hip-Hop's First Decade.
 By Jim Fricke and Charlie Ahearn. Published by Da Capo Press, a
 division of the Perseus Books Group. 2002.

a

A

A&R are bar bazaar bizarre car caviar cigar czar disbar far guitar jar par radar
scar sitar spar star tar

abc-ya duh extra Oprah zebra

ability (see *be*)

able cable disable enable fable label sable stable table unable unstable

abolish demolish polish tallish

abort (see **court**)

about boy scout blow-out bout clout devout doubt flout gout lout out pout
roundabout route scout shout snout spout sprout stout tout trout
wash-out worn-out

above dove glove ladylove love mourning dove of shove turtle dove

absolute (see **cute**)

abstract (see **act**)

absurd bird blackbird bluebird curd heard herd hummingbird ladybird
mockingbird overheard third word yellowbird

abuse accuse confuse cues deduce diffuse disuse duce excuse induce
infuse introduce juice misuse obtuse peruse produce profuse reduce
refuse reproduce seduce Syracuse use

abyss amiss analysis armistice bliss carcass cowardice dis dismiss emphasis
gangstress hiss hypothesis kiss miss mistress nemesis office
prejudice Swiss synthesis this

academic endemic epidemic polemic systematic (see *tick*)

accelerate (see **ate**)

accept adept crept except intercept kept overslept slept stepped swept wept

access (see **confess**)

account amount count dismount fount mount paramount tantamount

accuse (see **abuse**)

ace base bass brace case chase commonplace debase disgrace displace
embrace encase erase face grace lace mace misplace pace place
race replace space steeplechase trace unlace vase

ace-deuce caboose juice goose loose moose noose papoose recluse
spruce truce vamoose

ache bake brake break cake fake flake forsake headache heartache
keepsake make mistake opaque quake rake sake shake snake stake
steak take wake

achy flaky quaky shaky snaky

achieve believe bereave conceive disbelieve eve grieve heave leave perceive receive relieve reprieve retrieve sleeve weave

acquire amplifier aspire attire buyer choir conspire crier cryer desire dire dryer entire esquire expire fire flier friar higher hire inquire inspire justifier liar magnifier multiplier mystifier perspire prior prophesier require retire satisfier sire squire supplier testifier tire transpire wire

acre baker breaker dressmaker faker heartbreaker maker matchmaker pacemaker peacemaker Quaker shaker strikebreaker taker troublemaker undertaker watchmaker

acrobat (see **at**)

acrobatic (see **attic**)

across albatross boss cross double-cross floss hoss gloss loss moss rhinoceros sauce toss

act abstract attract backed compact contract distract exact fact impact intact jacked packed pact protract racked react slacked smacked snacked subtract tact tracked tract

action abstraction attraction distraction extraction faction fraction reaction satisfaction subtraction traction transaction

active attractive extractive inactive proactive radioactive reactive

actor benefactor contractor detractor distracter extractor factor raptor reactor refractor tractor

actual contractual factual

ad (see **bad**)

add (see **bad**)

addict conflict constrict contradict convict derelict evict flicked inflict licked predict pricked strict

addiction affliction benediction contradiction conviction crucifixion depiction diction eviction fiction friction jurisdiction prediction restriction

addy caddie daddy fatty maddy natty patty

adjourn (see **learn**)

adjust (see **trust**)

admire acquire amplifier aspire attire buyer choir conspire crier cryer desire dire dryer entire esquire expire fire flier friar higher hire inquire inspire justifier liar magnifier multiplier mystifier perspire prior prophesier require retire satisfier sire squire supplier testifier tire transpire wire

a

admission (see **tradition**)

adopt copped flopped mopped opt popped stopped

adventure denture indenture misadventure venture

advice concise device dice entice ice lice mice nice paradise precise price
rice sacrifice spice splice suffice thrice twice vice

advocate (see **ate**)

affair (see **air**)

affect (see **defect**)

affection bisection circumspection collection complexion connection
correction defection deflection detection direction disaffection
dissection ejection election erection imperfection infection inflection
inspection intersection introspection objection perfection projection
protection reflection rejection resurrection retrospection section
selection vivisection

afford aboard accord award board bored ford harpsichord hoard lord
overboard poured reward shuffleboard soared sword ward

afraid aid arcade barricade blade blockade braid brayed brigade charade
crusade degrade dismayed dissuade down-grade escapade evade
fade grade grenade hayed invade laid lemonade made maid
masquerade paid parade persuade played promenade raid renegade
serenade shade spade stockade suede tirade trade

after grafter hereafter laughter rafter thereafter

afternoon (see **moon**)

again abstain airplane arraign ascertain attain brain Cain campaign cane
chain champagne cocaine complain contain crane detain disdain
domain drain entertain explain feign gain grain humane hurricane
hydroplane insane lane main Maine maintain mane migraine obtain
ordain pain pane pertain plain plane profane propane rain refrain
reign rein remain sane slain Spain sprain stain strain sustain train
vain vane vein wane windowpane (see *win*)

against condensed fenced sensed

age cage gage page rampage sage stage wage

agony (see **be**)

aggie (see **be**)

agree (see **be**)

ailment curtailment impalement implement

aim acclaim became blame came claim exclaim fame flame frame game
inflame lame maim name proclaim same shame tame

a

ain't acquaint complaint faint paint quaint restraint saint taint 'tain't

air affair anywhere aware bare bear billionaire blare care chair compare dare
debonair declare despair disrepair elsewhere everywhere fair fare
flair glare hair hare heir impair legionnaire mare midair millionaire
nightmare pair pare pear Pierre prayer prepare rare ready-to-wear
repair scare snare solitaire somewhere spare square stair stare swear
tear their there thoroughfare unaware underwear unfair ware wear
where

aisle (see **smile**)

AK (see **say**)

alarm arm charm disarm farm forearm harm

album aquarium auditorium become bum burdensome Christendom
come cranium crematorium crumb curriculum drum dumb
emporium fee-fi-fo-fum glum gum gymnasium hum kettledrum
kingdom martyrdom maximum meddlesome medium millennium
minimum mum museum numb opium overcome pendulum
petroleum platinum plum premium quarrelsome radium random
rum sanitarium scum slum some strum succumb sum swum tedium
thumb Tom Thumb Tweedledum uranium worrisome yum

ale bail bale blackmail Braille cocktail curtail exhale fail female flail frail hail
hale impale inhale jail mail male nail pale prevail rail regale sail sale
scale shale snail stale tail they'll veil whale

alert (see **hurt**)

alibi (see **cry**)

alimony acrimony baloney bony crony macaroni matrimony patrimony
phony pony sanctimony stony testimony Tony

all ball bawl brawl call crawl doll drawl enthrall fall gall haul install mall maul
Montreal nightfall overhaul parasol pitfall protocol rainfall scrawl
shawl small snowfall sprawl stall tall thrall wall waterfall y'all

allege dredge edge fledge hedge ledge privilege sacrilege sledge wedge

alley dilly-dally rally Sally tally valley

allow avow bough bow brow chow cow disavow endow frau how kowtow
now ow plough plow row slough somehow sow thou vow wow

allude (see **feud**)

allure (see **cure**)

almighty Aphrodite flighty mightily righty

alone atone backbone baritone blown bone chaperone clone condone
cone cornerstone cyclone flown full-blown full-grown gramophone

a

grindstone groan grown headstone known k-tone loan lone
microphone milestone moan monotone mown overgrown
overthrown own phone postpone prone saxophone sewn shown
stone telephone thrown tone trombone unknown xylophone zone

along belong bong ding-dong gong Hong Kong long ping-pong prong song
strong throng wrong

altar alter defaulter falter Gibraltar halter psalter

always hallways small ways (see *way*)

am Amsterdam anagram Birmingham cam clam cram dam damn
diaphragm fam gram ham jam lamb ma'am madame scram sham
slam swam telegram tram yam

amateur (see **her**)

amaze ablaze appraise bays blaze braze craze days daze faze gaze glaze
graze haze malaise mayonnaise maze nays nowadays plays praise ways

amble gamble ramble scramble shamble

amen citizen den fen hen hydrogen Ken men oxygen pen regimen
specimen ten then yen Zen

among (see **young**)

amorous clamorous glamorous (see *us*)

amount account count dismount fount mount paramount tantamount

amp camp champ clamp cramp damp lamp ramp stamp vamp

analysis catalysis dialysis paralysis (see *miss*)

anchor banker canker flanker franker rancor ranker spanker tanker thank 'er

and band brand canned command contraband demand expand fanned
grand hand land panned planned reprimand Rio Grande sand stand

angelic relic

angle dangle entangle jangle mangle spangle strangle tangle triangle
wrangle

anguish languish

anniversary cursory nursery (see **be**)

annoy (see **boy**)

annual manual

another brother mother other smother

ant aunt can't chant decant enchant grant implant plant rant scant shan't
slant transplant

anxiety impropriety notoriety piety propriety sobriety society variety (see **be**)

any Benny Jenny many penny

a

anyone begun bun comparison done everyone fun Galveston gun hon
Hun jettison none nun oblivion one outdone outrun overdone
overrun phenomenon pun run shotgun shun simpleton skeleton son
stun sun ton unison venison won

anything (see **sing**)

apart art cart chart counterpart dart depart heart mart part smart start
sweetheart tart upstart

ape cape cityscape drape escape grape landscape rape seascape shape tape

apologize (see **lies**)

apostle colossal docile fossil jostle

appalled bald scald

appear (see **near**)

appearance adherence clearance coherence disappearance incoherence
interference perseverance

applaud abroad awed broad clod cod defraud façade fraud God guffawed
Izod nod odd pod prod promenade quad rod roughshod shod sod
squad trod wad

applauding defrauding lauding marauding plodding prodding

applause because cause clause claws gauze laws menopause Oz pause
paws Santa Claus was

apple chapel dapple grapple scrapple

appliance alliance compliance defiance reliance

appreciate (see **ate**)

apprehensive comprehensive defensive expensive extensive
incomprehensive inexpensive intensive offensive pensive

approach broach coach cockroach encroach poach reproach roach

approve behoove disapprove disprove groove improve move
prove remove

arbor barber harbor (see *door*)

arcade (see **afraid**)

arch march parch starch

are A&R bar bazaar bizarre car caviar cigar czar disbar far guitar jar par radar
scar sitar spar star tar

area Bulgaria malaria

arena Athena concertina karena hyena subpoena Tina

argument (see **bent**)

aristocrat (see **at**)

a

aristocratic (see **attic**)

ark aardvark arc bark dark embark hark lark mark narc park patriarch remark
        shark spark stark

arm alarm charm disarm farm forearm harm

aroma coma diploma sarcoma Sonoma Tacoma

around (see **found**)

arrange change derange estrange exchange range strange

arrow barrow harrow marrow narrow sparrow tarot

art apart cart chart counterpart dart depart heart mart part smart start
        sweetheart tart upstart

article particle

artificial beneficial initial judicial official sacrificial superficial

ash balderdash bash brash cash clash crash dash flash gash gnash lash
        mash rash rehash slash smash splash stash thrash trash

ask bask cask flask mask masque task

ass (see **class**)

assault cobalt exalt fault halt malt salt somersault vault

assistant consistent distant existent inconsistent insistent persistent
        resistant subsistent

asteroid avoid alkaloid joyed Lloyd Sigmund Freud tabloid toyed void

at acrobat aristocrat autocrat bat brat bureaucrat cat chat democrat diplomat
        drat fat flat gat gnat hat mat pat phat rat rat-a-tat-tat sat scat spat stat
        thermostat vat

ate *one syllable:*
        bait crate date eight hate late mate plate rate skate slate state
        straight strait trait wait weight
        two syllables:
        await berate debate dictate donate equate estate frustrate irate
        locate narrate ornate placate relate rotate sedate translate vacate
        three syllables:
        abdicate advocate aggravate agitate amputate animate annotate
        arbitrate assimilate calculate candidate captivate celebrate circulate
        compensate complicate concentrate confiscate congratulate
        consecrate consolidate constipate consummate contaminate
        contemplate cooperate coordinate correlate culminate cultivate
        decimate decorate dedicate demonstrate desecrate designate
        detonate devastate dislocate dissipate dominate duplicate educate
        elevate estimate excavate fabricate fascinate fluctuate formulate

generate graduate gravitate habituate heavyweight hesitate hibernate illustrate imitate implicate incubate innovate inordinate insulate isolate legislate levitate liberate liquidate lubricate magistrate marinate mediate mitigate moderate modulate motivate nominate operate orchestrate oscillate overate overstate overweight penetrate perpetrate populate punctuate radiate regulate reinstate renovate ruminate saturate second-rate separate simulate situate speculate stimulate stipulate suffocate tabulate terminate titillate tolerate underrate understate underweight vacillate validate vegetate ventilate vindicate violate

four or more syllables:

accelerate accentuate accommodate accumulate affiliate alienate annihilate appreciate articulate assassinate associate collaborate commemorate commiserate communicate conciliate corroborate decapitate deliberate depreciate deteriorate discriminate elaborate eliminate emancipate emulate enunciate eradicate evacuate evaluate evaporate excommunicate exonerate extenuate exterminate facilitate humiliate illuminate incapacitate incarcerate incorporate incriminate inculcate infatuate impersonate insinuate intimidate intoxicate invigorate manipulate necessitate negotiate obliterate originate participate pontificate precipitate procrastinate reciprocate regurgitate rehabilitate reiterate rejuvenate resuscitate retaliate reverberate subordinate (see *deviate*)

athlete (see **sweet**)

athletic aesthetic alphabetic apathetic apologetic arithmetic cosmetic electromagnetic energetic frenetic genetic pathetic poetic sympathetic synthetic theoretic

atomic anatomic comic economic

attach batch catch detach dispatch hatch latch match patch scratch snatch

attack (see **back**)

attempt contempt dreamt exempt tempt unkempt

attend (see **friend**)

attention abstention apprehension ascension comprehension condescension convention dissension detention dimension dissension extension intention intervention invention mention retention suspension tension

attentive inattentive incentive inventive retentive

a

attic acrobatic aristocratic aromatic autocratic bureaucratic chromatic cinematic climactic democratic dogmatic dramatic erratic fanatic melodramatic operatic pragmatic problematic static stigmatic systematic thematic traumatic

attitude gratitude latitude platitude

attorney journey tourney (see *be*)

attractive active extractive inactive proactive radioactive reactive

audi (see *be*)

audition (see **tradition**)

autumn bottom

avenue (see **knew**)

avoid alkaloid asteroid joyed Lloyd Sigmund Freud tabloid toyed void

award (see **lord**)

aware (see **air**)

awe Arkansas awe bra caw claw draw flaw gnaw guffaw hurrah jaw law Ma nah outlaw overdraw Pa paw raw saw seesaw shah slaw squaw straw thaw withdraw

awesome blossom possum (see *some*)

awful lawful

awhile (see **smile**)

ax backs fax jacks lax max relax packs Saks sax slacks tax wax

I think it is important to look good and to dance, but I think it's more important to be a true artist than a half-talent, because beauty fades. There are millions of beautiful people in the world. There have been millions of beautiful bands that have come and gone, but if you don't have any substance and talent behind it, then after one or two albums there's another beautiful band there to take your place.

—Beyoncé Knowles of Destiny's Child

B

babble dabble rabble scrabble

baby maybe (see *be*)

bachelor (see **door**)

back almanac attack black Cadillac cardiac clickety-clack egomaniac feedback hack Hackensack haystack jack kleptomaniac knack lack Mack maniac pack plaque Pontiac Prozac quack rack sack shack slack snack stack tack track whack yak zodiac

bacon (see **taken**)

bad ad add Brad cad Chad clad Dad egad fad glad grad had lad nomad pad plaid sad shad Trinidad

baffle raffle snaffle

bag brag do-rag drag flag gag hag lag mag nag rag sag shag slag snag stag swag tag wag

bait (see **ate**)

balcony (see **be**)

bald appalled scald

bale ale bail blackmail Braille cocktail curtail exhale female flail frail hail hale impale inhale jail mail male nail pale prevail

ball all bawl b-ball brawl call crawl doll drawl fall gall haul install mall maul Montreal nightfall overhaul parasol pitfall protocol rainfall scrawl shawl small snowfall sprawl stall tall thrall wall waterfall y'all

ballad invalid salad valid

balloon (see **moon**)

banana (see **nirvana**)

band and bland brand canned command contraband demand expand fanned grand hand land panned planned reprimand Rio Grande sand stand

bandstand grandstand handstand

bang boomerang clang dang fang gang-bang hang orangutan rang sang slang sprang

bank blank clank crank dank drank flank frank Hank jank outrank plank prank rank sank shank shrank skank spank stank tank thank yank

banker anchor canker flanker franker rancor ranker spanker tanker thank 'er

bar A&R are bar bazaar bizarre car caviar cigar czar disbar far guitar jar par radar scar sitar spar star tar

B

barb garb

barber arbor harbor (see *door*)

barf scarf snarf

barge charge discharge enlarge large

bark aardvark arc ark dark embark hark lark mark narc park patriarch remark
shark spark stark

barn darn yarn

barracuda Bermuda Buddha gouda

barrage camouflage garage entourage mirage

barrel apparel carol

barrier carrier terrier (see *her*)

base (see **ace**)

bash ash balderdash brash cash clash crash dash flash gash gnash lash
mash rash rehash slash smash splash stash thrash trash

bashment cement comment convent consent content descent event
frequent meant percent present prevent relent repent resent torment
unbent well-meant (see *bent*)

basket casket gasket (see *it, get*)

baste aftertaste braced chaste distaste faced freckle-faced haste hatchet-
faced lambaste paste taste two-faced waist waste

bat (see *at*)

batch attach catch detach dispatch hatch latch match patch scratch snatch

bath aftermath homeopath math path psychopath sociopath wrath

battery flattery (see *be*)

battle cattle chattel embattle prattle rattle Seattle tattle

bay (see **say**)

b-ball (see **ball**)

b-boy (see **boy**)

be   *one syllable:*
bee fee flea flee free gee glee he key knee me plea pea sea see
she tea thee tree we wee ye
two syllables:
agree Audi CB debris decree degree foresee homey goatee GP
Gumby hee-hee Marie R&D theory trustee wintry
three syllables:
absentee agency agony amnesty ancestry archery armory artistry
bakery balcony battery bigotry blasphemy botany bourgeoisie bravery

B

brevity bribery burglary Calgary Calvary casualty cavity century certainty charity chastity chickadee chimpanzee chivalry clemency colony comedy company courtesy CPT crudity cruelty custody decency deputy destiny devotee diary dignity disagree DMZ drapery dynasty Eazy-E ebony ecstasy effigy elegy embassy employee enemy energy eulogy factory fallacy family fantasy felony fertility fiery first-degree flagrancy flattery fluency forgery frequency gaiety galaxy Galilee gallantry gallery Germany gravity guarantee harmony heresy hierarchy history homily honesty imagery industry infamy infancy infantry injury inquiry irony Italy ivory jamboree jealousy jeopardy jewelry jubilee legacy leniency levity liberty liturgy lottery loyalty lunacy luxury melody memory mercury mimicry ministry misery mockery modesty mutiny mystery nominee nursery odyssey oversee pageantry papacy parody paternity pedantry pedigree penalty perjury Ph.D. piety piracy pleasantry poetry poignancy policy potpourri poverty privacy prodigy property puberty purity quackery quality quantity rarity recipe rectory referee refugee remedy repartee revelry rhapsody rickety rivalry robbery rosemary royalty salary sanctity sanity savagery savory scarcity scenery scrutiny secrecy sesame shadowy shivery silvery simile slavery slippery sorcery strategy subsidy subtlety sugary summary symmetry sympathy symphony tapestry tendency Tennessee thievery timpani treachery trickery trilogy trinity truancy tyranny unity urgency victory watery witchery

four or more syllables:

ability absurdity activity actuality adversity affinity agility ambiguity amenity animosity anarchy anatomy anniversary anonymity antiquity anxiety artillery astrology astronomy atrocity audacity authenticity authority barbarity biography biology brilliancy brutality capacity captivity celebrity Christianity chronology combustibility commodity community compatibility complacency complexity complimentary comprehensibility conformity consistency conspiracy contradictory criminality curiosity debauchery deformity delivery dependency depravity diversity diplomacy directory discovery discrepancy divinity eccentricity economy efficiency electricity elementary emergency enormity epitome equality eternity expectancy extremity facility facsimile ferocity festivity fiddle-de-dee fidelity formality fraternity frivolity futility generosity geography geometry gratuity heredity hilarity hospitably hostility humanity humility hypocrisy identity idiocy illiteracy immodesty immunity inability incapacity inconsistency indecency individuality inferiority infirmary infirmity ingenuity

B

inhumanity insufficiency insurgency integrity intensity legality
longevity machinery mahogany majesty maternity maturity mediocrity
minority mobility monogamy monopoly monstrosity morality
mythology nationality nativity necessity neutrality nobility notoriety
peculiarity personality philanthropy philosophy photography popularity
pornography posterity prosperity priority profanity proficiency
promiscuity propriety proximity psychiatry publicity reality recovery
rudimentary satisfactory security sensibility sensuality sentimentality
serenity severity sexuality similarity simplicity sincerity society sophistry
spontaneity stability sterility stupidity subjectively superficiality
superiority technicality theology totality tranquillity triviality uniformity
university utility validity variety velocity virginity vulgarity

beach breach each impeach leech peach preach reach screech speech teach

bean (see **mean**)

beard appeared cleared disappeared feared jeered neared persevered
smeared speared weird

beast ceased creased deceased east feast least pieced priest yeast

beat athlete beet bittersweet bleat cheat compete complete conceit
concrete deceit defeat delete deplete discreet discrete eat elite feat
feet fleet greet heat incomplete indiscreet meat meet mistreat neat
obsolete parakeet receipt repeat retreat seat sheet sleet street suite
sweet treat wheat

beaten cheatin' Cretan eaten Eton meetin' sweeten unbeaten

beautiful dutiful full (see *wool*)

beauty cutie duty patootie (see **be**)

became (see **aim**)

because applause cause clause claws gauze laws menopause Oz pause
paws Santa Claus was

become (see **dumb**)

bed ahead bedspread bread bred coed dead dread fed figurehead fled
flowerbed fountainhead gingerbread head inbred lead led misled
misread overfed read red riverbed said shed shred sled sped spread
thoroughbred thread underfed unthread wed

beef belief brief chief disbelief grief leaf reef relief thief

been again aspirin begin Berlin bin chagrin chin Crooklyn discipline
feminine fin 5x10 genuine gin grin heroine in inn kin mandolin
mannequin masculine moccasin origin pin saccharine shin sin skin
spin thick-and-thin thin tin twin violin win within

beer adhere appear atmosphere auctioneer bombardier career cashier cavalier chandelier cheer clear dear deer disappear ear engineer fear financier frontier gear hear hemisphere here insincere interfere jeer lavaliere leer mere mountaineer near overhear overseer peer persevere pioneer queer racketeer reappear rear revere seer severe shear sheer sincere smear sneer spear sphere stratosphere tear veneer volunteer year

before abhor ambassador ashore auditor bachelor Baltimore boar bore chancellor chore commodore competitor conspirator contributor core corps corridor deplore dinosaur door drawer Ecuador editor emperor encore evermore explore exterior floor folklore for fore four furthermore galore governor ignore implore inferior lore matador metaphor more nevermore nor oar offshore or orator ore poor pour rapport restore roar score seashore senator señor shore Singapore snore soar sophomore sore spore store swore therefore Thor tore troubadour underscore uproar visitor whore yore your

beg egg keg leg peg

begin again aspirin been Berlin bin chagrin chin Crooklyn discipline feminine fin 5x10 genuine gin grin heroine in inn kin mandolin mannequin masculine moccasin origin pin saccharine shin sin skin spin thick-and-thin thin tin twin violin win within

beginner B.F. Skinner breadwinner dinner inner sinner skinner spinner thinner winner

begun anyone bun comparison everyone fun Galveston gun hon Hun jettison none nun oblivion one outdone outrun overdone overrun phenomenon pun run shotgun shun simpleton skeleton son stun sun ton unison venison won

behavior misbehavior savior

being agreeing decreeing disagreeing farseeing fleeing foreseeing freeing guaranteeing overseeing seeing teeing unseeing

belch squelch welch

belief beef brief chief disbelief grief leaf relief thief

believe achieve bereave conceive disbelieve eve grieve heave leave perceive receive relieve reprieve retrieve sleeve weave

bell belle caramel Carmel carrousel cell clientele dell dwell excel farewell fell gel hell hotel infidel knell mademoiselle personnel sell shell smell spell tell well yell

belly celly deli jelly Kelly Nelly Shelly smelly

B

belong along belong bong ding-dong gong Hong Kong long ping-pong
prong song strong throng wrong

below (see **blow**)

belt Celt dealt felt heartfelt melt pelt welt

bench clench drench French monkey wrench quench stench trench
wench wrench

bend (see **friend**)

Benjamin(s) aspirin been begin Berlin bin chagrin chin discipline feminine
fin 5x10 genuine grin heroine in inn kin mandolin mannequin
masculine moccasin origin pin saccharine shin sin skin spin thick-
and-thin thin tin twin violin win within

beneath heath teeth underneath wreath

beneficial artificial initial judicial official sacrificial superficial

bent

one syllable:
cent dent gent Lent lent rent sent spent tent vent went

two syllables:
accent assent cement comment convent consent content descent
event fluent frequent meant percent present prevent relent repent
resent torment unbent well-meant

three syllables:
accident affluent president prominent punishment regiment
represent resident reverent sacrament sediment sentiment
settlement subsequent succulent supplement temperament
tenement testament tournament violent wonderment

four or more syllables:
abandonment acknowledgment advertisement benevolent
bewilderment coincident development disarmament embarrassment
embellishment embezzlement embodiment encouragement
enlightenment environment establishment experiment imprisonment
incompetent ingredient intelligent intent invent irreverent malevolent
misrepresent predicament replenishment self-confident sentiment
settlement succulent supplement temperament tenement testament
tournament violent wonderment

Bentley (see **be**)

berry adversary airy arbitrary beneficiary bury canary capillary cautionary
commentary culinary customary dairy dictionary dietary dignitary
disciplinary discretionary evolutionary extraordinary fairy February ferry

functionary hairy hereditary honorary imaginary incendiary intermediary January Jerry legendary legionary literary luminary Mary mercenary military momentary monetary mortuary necessary obituary ordinary planetary prairie proprietary pulmonary reactionary revolutionary sanctuary sanitary scary secretary seminary sherry solitary stationary temporary Terry very visionary vocabulary voluntary wary

best arrest attest blessed breast Bucharest Budapest chest congest contest crest detest digest divest dressed guessed guest infest ingest interest invest jest manifest messed molest nest pest protest request rest second-best suggest test unrest vest zest

bet (see **met**)

Bethlehem condemn Eminem gem hem phlegm requiem stem them

better debtor cheddar getter letter setter sweater wetter (see *her*)

beyond blond bond correspond dawned fond pond respond spawned vagabond wand yawned

bible libel tribal

bid did forbid grid hid invalid lid Madrid pyramid rid skid slid squid

big dig fig gig jig pig rig swig thingamajig twig wig underdig

bigot spigot

bike hike like mike spike strike tyke

biker hiker piker spiker striker (see *her*)

bill (see **fill**)

bingo dingo flamingo gringo jingo lingo (see *glow*)

bird absurd blackbird bluebird curd heard herd hummingbird ladybird mockingbird overheard third word yellowbird

birth dearth earth girth mirth worth

biscuit brisket (see *it*)

bitch bewitch ditch enrich glitch hitch pitch rich snitch stitch switch twitch which

bite (see **night**)

bitter counterfeiter critter fitter fritter glitter litter quitter sitter transmitter twitter (see *her*)

bizarre A&R are bar bazaar car caviar cigar czar disbar far guitar jar par radar scar sitar spar star tar

blab cab crab dab drab fab gab grab jab lab nab scab slab stab tab

blade (see **afraid**)

B

blame acclaim aim became came claim exclaim fame flame frame game inflame lame maim name proclaim same shame tame

blank bank clank crank dank drank flank frank Hank jank outrank plank prank rank sank shank shrank skank spank stank tank thank yank

blast aghast cast classed contrast fast flabbergast forecast gassed last mast outlast overcast passed past vast

blatant latent patent

blaze ablaze amaze appraise bays braze craze days daze faze gaze glaze graze haze malaise mayonnaise maze nays nowadays plays praise ways

blazer appraiser gazer laser maser phaser praiser razor stargazer

bleed agreed breed centipede concede creed deed exceed feed greed heed inbreed knead lead mislead need precede proceed read recede reed secede seed speed stampede succeed Swede tweed weed

blend (see **friend**)

bless (see **confess**)

blind behind bind find grind hind humankind kind mastermind mind remind signed unkind unwind wind wined

blinded evil-minded feebleminded like-minded minded narrow-minded reminded

bling-bling (see **ring**)

blink brink chink clink drink fink ink kink link mink pink rink shrink sink slink stink think wink zinc

bliss abyss amiss analysis armistice carcass cowardice dis dismiss emphasis gangstress hiss hypothesis kiss miss mistress nemesis office prejudice Swiss synthesis this

blister assister mister resister sister twister (see *her*)

blizzard gizzard lizard scissored wizard

bloat (see **boat**)

blond (see **beyond**)

blood bud cud dud flood mud scud spud stud thud

bloom boom broom cloakroom doom entomb flume gloom groom room tomb whom womb zoom

blossom awesome possum (see *some*)

blouse douse grouse house louse madhouse mouse outhouse penthouse slaughterhouse souse spouse

blow afro although banjo beau below bestow bow buffalo bungalow calico crossbow crow depot doe domino dough embryo escrow Eskimo

flow foe forgo fro gazebo gigolo glow go grow heigh-ho ho-ho hobo
hoe incognito indigo Joe know long ago low Mexico mistletoe mow
no oboe oh outgrow overflow overgrow overthrow owe Pinocchio
plateau quo rainbow ratio roe row sew show slow snow so Soho
status quo stow studio though throw tiptoe to-and-fro toe Tokyo tow
tremolo undergo undertow vertigo woe yo yo-yo

blown (see **known**)

blue (see **do**)

blues booze bruise choose cruise lose news ooze snooze whose

bluff buff cuff duff enough fluff gruff huff muff powder puff rough scruff
scuff snuff stuff tough

blunder plunder under thunder wonder

blunt affront bunt confront forefront front grunt hunt punt runt shunt stunt

blur (see **her**)

BMX decks duplex DMX ex flex hex Lex necks pecks reflex Rolodex sex
specs Tex unisex

board (see **lord**)

boast coast foremost furthermost ghost host innermost most post roast
toast whipping post

boat afloat antidote bloat c-note coat connote denote dote float footnote
gloat goat misquote moat note oat overcoat promote quote remote
riverboat rote smote throat tote turncoat underwrote vote wrote

body embody gaudy lawdy nobody shoddy somebody toddy

bogard avant-garde card chard discard disregard guard hard lard regard
retard tarred yard

bold behold blindfold centerfold cold fold foothold foretold gold hold
household marigold mold old retold scold sold told uphold withhold

bolt colt dolt jolt revolt thunderbolt

bomb aplomb calm embalm Guam Mom palm psalm qualm

bombard avant-garde bogard card chard discard disregard guard hard lard
regard retard tarred yard

bomber calmer embalmer palmer (see *her*)

bond beyond blond correspond fond dawned pond respond spawned
vagabond wand yawned

bone alone atone backbone baritone blown chaperone clone condone
cone cornerstone cyclone flown full-blown full-grown gramophone
grindstone groan grown headstone k-tone loan lone microphone
milestone moan monotone mown overgrown overthrown own

B

phone postpone prone saxophone sewn shown stone telephone thrown tone trombone unknown xylophone zone

book brook cook crook hook look mistook nook outlook rook shook took undertook

boom bloom broom cloakroom doom entomb flume gloom groom room tomb whom womb zoom

boost roost

booth couth Duluth sleuth tooth truth uncouth youth

booty cootie fruity snooty tutti-frutti

booze blues bruise choose cruise lose news ooze snooze whose

boozer accuser amuser cruiser lose 'er loser muser oozer refuser snoozer user (see *her*)

border boarder disorder hoarder order recorder

born adorn airborne Cape Horn Capricorn corn horn lovelorn Matterhorn morn mourn popcorn scorn stillborn sworn unicorn warn worn

borrow morrow sorrow tomorrow

botch blotch crotch debauch hopscotch notch Scotch watch wristwatch

both growth loath oath overgrowth undergrowth

bottle dottle mottle throttle waddle wattle

bottom autumn

bought astronaut brought caught cosmonaut fought naught ought overwrought sought taught thought wrought

bounce announce counts denounce mounts ounce pounce pronounce renounce trounce

bound (see **found**)

boundary foundry

bout about boy scout blow-out clout devout doubt flout gout lout out pout roundabout route scout shout snout spout sprout stout tout trout wash-out worn-out

bow (see **blow**)

bowl (see **control**)

box chickenpox e-box equinox fox mailbox orthodox ox paradox socks stocks rocks Xerox

boy annoy convoy corduroy coy decoy destroy employ enjoy homeboy Illinois joy ploy Roy Savoy soy toy troy

brag bag do-rag drag flag gag hag lag mag nag rag sag shag slag snag stag swag tag wag

B

bragger bagger carpetbagger dagger stagger swagger tagger
brain (see **chain**)
branch avalanche ranch
brand and band canned command contraband demand expand fanned
         grand hand land panned planned reprimand Rio Grande sand stand
brandy Andy candy dandy handy randy sandy
brass (see **class**)
brat (see **at**)
brave behave cave concave crave engrave forgave gave grave knave pave
         rave save shave slave waive wave
bravery savory slavery
bread ahead bed bedspread bred coed dead dread fed figurehead fled
         flowerbed fountainhead gingerbread head inbred lead led misled
         misread overfed read red riverbed said shed shred sled sped spread
         thoroughbred thread underfed unthread wed
breadline headline deadline
break ache bake brake cake fake flake forsake headache heartache
         keepsake make mistake opaque quake rake sake shake snake stake
         steak take wake
breakup make-up shake-up take up wake up
bribe circumscribe describe jibe prescribe scribe subscribe tribe vibe
brick arithmetic arsenic candlestick candlewick Catholic chick click copasetic
         flick heartsick hick kick lick limerick love-sick lunatic maverick medic
         nick pick sick slick stick thick tic tick wick
bride beside bona fide collide confide countryside decide defied died
         dignified divide eyed fireside guide hide hillside homicide inside lied
         outside override pride provide reside ride side slide snide stride
         subdivide subside suicide tide tried wide yuletide
bridge abridge fridge ridge
bright (see **flight**)
brilliant resilient
bring (see **sing**)
broke artichoke baroque bloke choke cloak coke croak evoke folk invoke
         joke oak poke provoke revoke smoke soak spoke stroke toke woke
         yoke
broth cloth froth moth swath wroth
brother another mother other smother

B

brought (see **thought**)

brown clown crown down downtown drown frown gown hand-me-down lock-down noun Oaktown renown town tumble-down upside down uptown

brunch bunch crunch hunch lunch munch punch scrunch

brush blush crush flush gush lush mush plush rush slush thrush underbrush

brute (see **cute**)

bubble double rubble stubble trouble

buck (see **truck**)

bucket Nantucket (see *it*)

buckle Arbuckle chuckle honeysuckle knuckle suckle

Buddha Bermuda Buddha Gouda

budge drudge fudge grudge judge misjudge nudge smudge

buff (see **bluff**)

bug drug dug jug hug lug mug plug pug rug shrug slug smug snug thug tug

build chilled drilled filled guild killed rebuild willed

builder bewilder (see *her*)

built guilt hilt jilt kilt quilt spilt stilt tilt Vanderbilt wilt

bulge divulge indulge

bull cock-and-bull do-able full marble pull wool (see *beautiful*)

bum (see **dumb**)

bump chump clump dump hump jump lump plump rump slump stump thump trump ump

bunch brunch crunch hunch lunch munch punch scrunch

bungle jungle

bunny funny honey sunny

burial aerial

burn adjourn churn concern discern earn fern intern kern learn overturn return sojourn spurn stern taciturn turn urn yearn

burnt learnt weren't

burp chirp twerp usurp Wyatt Earp

burrow borough furrow thorough

burst cursed first nursed outburst thirst versed worst

bury (see **cherry**)

bus (see **us**)

bush cush push

bust (see **trust**)

bustle corpuscle hustle muscle mussel rustle tussle

busy dizzy frizzy Lizzie Tin Lizzie rizzi tizzy

but butt cut coconut glut gut halibut hut King Tut mutt nut putt rut scuttlebutt shut slut smut strut uncut

butler subtler

butter clutter cutter flutter gutter mutter putter shutter sputter strutter stutter utter

button cuttin' glutton guttin' mutton nuthin'

buzz abuzz buzz cause coz does fuzz was

by (see **bye**)

bye alibi amplify banzai barfly butterfly buy by certify clarify crucify cry defy deify deny die dignify diversify dragonfly drive-by dry dye eye firefly fly fry FYI glorify gratify guy high horrify I identify imply July justify lie lullaby modify my mystify notify passerby pie pry qualify rely rye satisfy sci-fi shy sigh signify simplify sky sly specify spry spy terrify testify thigh tie try underlie verify why

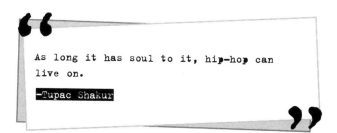

> As long it has soul to it, hip-hop can live on.
>
> —Tupac Shakur

C

C

cab blab crab dab drab fab gab grab jab lab nab scab slab stab tab
cabbage average ravage savage
cable (see **able**)
cad (see **bad**)
Caesar appeaser ease 'er freezer please 'er sees 'er seize 'er sleaze 'er
        squeeze 'er teaser
cage age gage page rampage sage stage wage
cake (see **fake**)
calf carafe epitaph giraffe graph paragraph phonograph photograph
        polygraph riffraff staff telegraph
call all ball bawl brawl crawl doll drawl fall gall haul install mall maul
        Montreal nightfall overhaul parasol pitfall protocol rainfall scrawl
        shawl small snowfall sprawl stall tall thrall wall waterfall y'all
calm aplomb bomb CD-ROM embalm Guam Mom palm psalm qualm
calmer bomber embalmer palmer
calorie gallery Mallory salary
camp amp champ clamp cramp damp lamp ramp stamp vamp
can ban can-can Dan fan Iran man Nan plan ran Tehran
can't ant aunt chant decant enchant grant implant plant rant scant shan't
        slant transplant
canal chorale gal morale pal shall
canary (see **cherry**)
candidate (see **ate**)
candle dandle handle sandal scandal vandal
candy Andy brandy dandy handy randy sandy
cap chap clap flap gap handicap lap map mishap nap rap sap scrap slap
        snap strap tap trap wrap zap
cap-cocked cocked crocked deadlocked defrocked flocked glocked grid
        locked hocked knocked locked mocked padlocked rocked shocked
        socked squawked stalked tomahawked unlocked
cape ape cityscape drape escape grape landscape rape seascape shape tape
captive adaptive (see *active*)
captivity (see **be**)
capture rapture recapture (see *your*)

car A&R are bar bazaar bizarre caviar cigar czar disbar far guitar jar par radar scar sitar spar star tar

carat carrot parrot

card avant-garde bogard bombard card discard disregard guard hard lard regard retard tarred yard

care affair air anywhere aware bare bear billionaire blare chair compare dare debonair declare despair disrepair elsewhere everywhere fair fare flair glare hair hare heir impair legionnaire mare midair millionaire nightmare pair pare pear Pierre prayer prepare rare ready-to-wear repair scare snare solitaire somewhere spare square stair stare swear tear their there thoroughfare unaware underwear unfair ware wear where

career (see **near**)

cargo argot embargo Fargo largo

carp harp sharp

carriage disparage marriage miscarriage

carry hare Kari marry miscarry parry vary (see *cherry*)

cart apart art chart counterpart dart depart heart mart part smart start sweetheart tart upstart

cartoon (see **moon**)

carve starve

case (see **ace**)

cash ash balderdash bash brash clash crash dash flash gash gnash rash rehash slash smash splash stash thrash trash

casino andantino bambino Filipino keno Reno

cask ask bask flask mask masque task

casket basket gasket (see *it, get*)

cast aghast blast classed contrast fast flabbergast forecast gassed last mast outlast overcast passed past vast

castle tassel vassal wrassle

casualty (see **be**)

cat (see **at**)

catch attach batch detach dispatch hatch latch match patch scratch snatch

catch etch fetch kvetch retch sketch stretch wretch

catcher dispatcher scratcher snatcher

Catholic (see **brick**)

cattle battle chattel embattle prattle rattle Seattle tattle

C

caught astronaut bought brought cosmonaut fought naught ought
    overwrought sought taught thought wrought

cause applause because clause claws gauze laws menopause Oz pause
    paws Santa Claus was

cave behave brave concave crave engrave forgave gave grave knave pave
    rave save shave slave waive wave

cavern tavern (see *burn*)

cavity depravity gravity

CB (see **be**)

celebrate (see **ate**)

cell bell belle caramel Carmel carrousel clientele dell dwell excel farewell
    fell gel hell hotel infidel knell mademoiselle personnel sell shell
    smell spell swell tell well yell

cellar dweller feller fortuneteller interstellar propeller Rockefeller seller
    smeller speller stellar teller

cello bellow delo fellow hello Jell-O mellow Othello yellow

celly belly deli jelly Kelly Nelly Shelly smelly

censor censer condenser denser dispenser fencer Spencer

cent (see **bent**)

center dissenter enter experimenter frequenter inventor mentor presenter
    preventer renter tormentor

chain abstain again airplane arraign ascertain attain brain Cain campaign
    cane champagne cocaine complain contain crane detain disdain
    domain drain entertain explain feign gain grain humane hurricane
    hydroplane insane lane main Maine maintain mane migraine obtain
    ordain pain pane pertain plain plane profane propane rain refrain
    reign rein remain sane slain Spain sprain stain strain sustain train
    vain vane vein windowpane

chair (see **air**)

chamber amateur blur chamber chauffeur concur confer connoisseur defer
    demur deter fur gangster her incur infer Jennifer myrrh occur per
    prefer purr

champ amp camp clamp cramp damp lamp ramp stamp vamp

champagne (see **chain**)

chance advance ants circumstance dance enhance extravagance finance
    France glance lance pants prance romance stance trance

change arrange derange estrange exchange range strange

C

channel flannel panel
chapel apple dapple grapple scrapple
charade (see **afraid**)
charge barge discharge enlarge large
charm arm alarm disarm farm forearm harm
chaste baste aftertaste braced distaste faced freckle-faced haste hatchet-faced lambaste paste taste waist waste
chat (see **at**)
chauffeur gopher loafer (see *her*)
cheap barkeep cheep creep deep heap keep leap peep reap seep sheep sleep steep sweep weep
cheat athlete beat beet bittersweet bleat compete complete conceit concrete deceit defeat delete deplete discreet discrete eat elite feat feet fleet greet heat incomplete indiscreet meat meet mistreat neat obsolete parakeet receipt repeat retreat seat sheet sleet street suite sweet treat wheat
cheated bleated competed completed conceited defeated deleted depleted excreted greeted heated maltreated pleated repeated retreated seated secreted sleeted treated
check Czech deck fleck heck neck peck Quebec speck trek wreck
cheddar better debtor getter setter sweater wetter (see *her*)
cheer adhere appear atmosphere auctioneer beer bombardier career cashier cavalier chandelier clear dear deer disappear ear engineer fear financier frontier gear hear hemisphere here insincere interfere jeer lavaliere leer mere mountaineer near overhear overseer peer persevere pioneer queer racketeer reappear rear revere seer severe shear sheer sincere smear sneer spear sphere stratosphere tear veneer volunteer year
cheese (see **ease**)
chef clef deaf
cherry adversary airy arbitrary beneficiary berry bury canary capillary cautionary commentary culinary customary dairy dictionary dietary dignitary disciplinary discretionary evolutionary extraordinary fairy February ferry functionary hairy hereditary honorary imaginary incendiary intermediary January Jerry legendary legionary literary luminary Mary mercenary military momentary monetary mortuary nary necessary obituary ordinary Perry planetary prairie proprietary pulmonary reactionary revolutionary sanctuary sanitary scary secretary

C

seminary sherry solitary stationary temporary Terry very visionary
vocabulary voluntary wary

chess (see **confess**)

chest arrest attest best blessed breast Bucharest Budapest congest contest
crest detest digest divest dressed guessed guest infest ingest interest
invest jest manifest messed molest nest pest protest request rest
second-best suggest test unrest vest zest

chew (see **knew**)

chick (see **brick**)

chicken quicken sicken stricken thicken (see *in*)

chief beef belief brief disbelief grief leaf relief thief

child dialed mild piled smiled wild

chill bill daffodil distill drill frill fulfill gill grill hill ill imbecile instill kill mill nil
quill shrill sill skill spill still swill thrill till trill until whippoorwill will
windmill windowsill

chilling (see **willing**)

chime climb crime dime I'm lime mime pantomime prime rhyme slime
show time summertime thyme time

chin (see **been**)

chip (see **trip**)

chirp burp chirp twerp usurp Wyatt Earp

chivalry delivery livery shivery slivery

choice invoice rejoice voice

choir (see **fire**)

choke artichoke baroque bloke broke cloak coke croak evoke folk invoke
joke oak poke provoke revoke smoke soak spoke stroke toke
woke yoke

choose blues booze bruise cruise lose news ooze snooze whose

chop (see **drop**)

chopper (see **proper**)

chore (see **door**)

chorus brontosaurus sonorous Taurus thesaurus (see *us*)

chose arose close compose decompose depose disclose dispose doze
enclose expose foreclose froze goes hose impose indispose knows
nose owes pose predispose presuppose prose rose suppose those
toes transpose woes

Christ diced heist iced zeitgeist

C

christen glisten listen

Christianity (see **be**)

Christmas isthmus (see *us*)

chrome chromosome comb dome foam gnome home honeycomb
metronome Nome poem roam Rome tome

chuckle Arbuckle buckle honeysuckle knuckle suckle

chunk bunk chunk cyberpunk drunk dunk flunk funk hunk junk monk
p-funk plunk punk shrunk skunk slunk spunk stunk sunk trunk

church besmirch birch lurch perch research search smirch

cigar A&R are bar bazaar bizarre car caviar czar disbar far guitar jar par radar
scar sitar spar star tar

cinch flinch inch lynch pinch

cinematic (see **attic**)

citizen amen den fen hen hydrogen Ken men oxygen pen regimen
specimen ten then yen Zen

city committee ditty gritty kitty pity pretty self-pity witty

civil drivel shrivel snivel swivel

clash ash balderdash bash brash cash clash crash flash gash gnash rash
rehash slash smash splash stash thrash trash

class alas amass ass bass brass crass gas glass grass harass hourglass lass
looking-glass mass morass mustache overpass pass sass surpass

claw Arkansas awe bra caw claw draw flaw gnaw guffaw hurrah jaw law Ma
nah outlaw overdraw Pa paw raw saw seesaw shah slaw squaw
straw thaw withdraw

clean bean between caffeine canteen chlorine codeine Colleen convene
cuisine dean demean evergreen foreseen gasoline Gene green
guillotine Halloween in-between intervene kerosene lean lien
machine marine mean Nazarene nectarine nicotine obscene preen
quarantine queen ravine routine sardine scene seen serene spleen
submarine tambourine tangerine teen thirteen (etc.) Vaseline
velveteen wintergreen wolverine 'zine

cleanse bends dens lens mends sends tends

clearance adherence appearance coherence disappearance incoherence
interference perseverance

clerk handiwork irk jerk Kirk lurk murk overwork perk quirk shirk smirk Turk work

clever endeavor ever forever however lever never sever whatever
whenever wherever whoever

client compliant defiant giant ignorant reliant self-reliant

cliff handkerchief if sniff stiff tiff whiff

climatic (see **attic**)

climb chime crime dime I'm lime mime pantomime prime rhyme slime
show time summertime thyme time

clock Bangkok beanstalk boondock cock cornstalk crock deadlock defrock
dock dreadlock flintlock flock frock gawk glock gridlock hawk hock
J. S. Bach jock knock Little Rock livestock lock mock Mohawk padlock
peacock rock shock sidewalk small talk Tupoc smock sock squawk
stalk stock talk tomahawk unlock walk wok

clog analog bog catalog cog fog demagogue dialogue dog epilogue flog frog
grog hog jog log monologue synagogue travelogue

close adios bellicose comatose diagnose dose engross grandiose gross
morose nose overdose varicose verbose

close arose chose compose decompose depose disclose dispose doze
enclose expose foreclose froze goes hose impose indispose knows
nose owes pose predispose presuppose prose rose suppose those
toes transpose woes

cloth broth froth moth swath wroth

cloud allowed aloud crowd enshroud loud plowed proud shroud
thundercloud

cloudy cum laude dowdy howdy rowdy

clover Dover drover moreover over rover (see *her*)

clown brown crown down downtown drown frown gown hand-me-down lock-
down noun Oaktown renown town tumble-down upside down uptown

club Beelzebub bub cub grub hub hubbub pub rub rub-a-dub-dub scrub
shrub snub stub sub tub

clue (see **do**)

clutch crutch Dutch hutch inasmuch much retouch such touch

c-note afloat antidote bloat boat c-note coat connote denote dote float
footnote gloat goat misquote moat note oat overcoat promote quote

coach approach broach cockroach encroach poach reproach roach

coal (see **control**)

coarse course divorce endorse force horse Norse reinforce remorse
resource source

coast boast foremost furthermost ghost host innermost most post roast
toast whipping post

coat (see **boat**)

coax folks hoax jokes smokes spokes yokes

cockroach approach broach coach encroach poach reproach roach

code (see **road**)

coffee toffee (see *me*)

coffin coughin' often soften

coherent adherent incoherent inherent perseverant

coil broil foil loyal oil recoil royal spoil toil turmoil

coin Des Moines groin join loin purloin sirloin tenderloin

coincidence (see **fence**)

cold behold blindfold bold centerfold fold foothold foretold gold hold
household marigold mold old retold scold sold told uphold withhold

collapse caps craps elapse flaps lapse maps naps perhaps saps traps wraps

collar bawler brawler call 'er caller choler crawler dollar hauler mauler
scrawler smaller squalor taller

collect (see **defect**)

collection (see **affection**)

college acknowledge knowledge (see *ledge*)

collision (see **vision**)

color discolor duller sculler Technicolor

coma aroma diploma sarcoma Sonoma Tacoma

comb chrome chromosome dome foam gnome home honeycomb
metronome Nome poem roam Rome tome

come album aquarium auditorium become bum burdensome Christendom
cranium crematorium crumb curriculum drum dumb emporium fee-
fi-fo-fum glum gum gymnasium hum kettledrum kingdom
martyrdom maximum meddlesome medium millennium minimum
mum museum numb opium overcome pendulum petroleum
platinum plum premium quarrelsome radium random rum
sanitarium scum slum some strum succumb sum swum tedium
thumb Tom Thumb Tweedledum uranium worrisome yum

comedy (see **be**)

comfort (see **court**)

comic atomic anatomic economic

commune attune dune immune impugn inopportune June tune
(see *moon*)

communicate (see **ate**)

company (see **be**)

complain (see **chain**)

complete athlete beat beet bittersweet bleat cheat complete conceit concrete deceit defeat delete deplete discreet discrete eat elite feat feet fleet greet heat incomplete indiscreet meat meet mistreat neat obsolete parakeet receipt repeat retreat seat sheet sleet street suite sweet treat wheat

complex BMX decks duplex DMX ex flex necks pecks reflex Rolodex specs Tex unisex

complexion (see **affection**)

complicate (see **ate**)

compliment (see **cent**)

compute (see **cute**)

computer (see **suitor**)

con Amazon autobahn Babylon bonbon Bonn brawn chiffon dawn drawn echelon fawn gone lawn neon on pawn pentagon silicon swan undergone upon wan woebegone wonton yawn

concentrate (see **ate**)

concern adjourn burn churn discern earn fern intern kern learn overturn return sojourn spurn stern taciturn turn urn yearn

concert (see **hurt**)

concrete (see **sweet**)

condemn Bethlehem Eminem gem hem phlegm requiem stem them

condition acquisition addition admission ambition ammunition attrition audition coalition commission competition composition definition demolition deposition disposition edition electrician emission exhibition expedition exposition extradition fission ignition imposition inhibition inquisition intermission intuition magician mathematician mission musician nutrition omission opposition partition permission petition physician politician position prohibition proposition recognition rendition repetition requisition statistician submission superstition technician tradition transmission transposition transition tuition (see *in*)

conduct abduct construct deduct instruct obstruct plucked viaduct

confess access address baroness bashfulness bitterness bless caress chess cleverness cloudiness compress craziness deadliness depress digress distress dizziness dress duress eagerness easiness eeriness emptiness excess express finesse foolishness guess happiness haziness homelessness idleness impress joyfulness laziness less

limitless Loch Ness lustfulness mess nervousness obsess openness
oppress outrageousness penniless playfulness possess press
progress queasiness recess regress repossess repress rockiness
seediness shallowness silkiness sleaziness sleepiness sneakiness
SOS spaciousness spitefulness stress success suppress
thoughtfulness transgress uselessness viciousness willingness
worldliness yes youthfulness

confession aggression compression concession depression digression
discretion expression impression indiscretion obsession oppression
possession procession profession progression recession regression
repression secession session succession suppression transgression

confetti fetti jetty machete petty spaghetti sweaty

confidential credential deferential differential essential existential
influential nonessential potential preferential presidential providential
prudential quintessential residential sequential torrential

conflict addict constrict contradict convict derelict evict flicked inflict licked
predict pricked strict

conform chloroform conform deform form inform norm perform rainstorm
reform snowstorm storm swarm transform uniform warm

confuse abuse accuse cues deduce diffuse disuse duce excuse induce
infuse introduce juice misuse obtuse peruse produce profuse reduce
refuse reproduce seduce Syracuse use

conquer conker honker (see *her*)

consist (see **exist**)

contain (see **chain**)

contribution (see *revolution*)

control bowl buttonhole cajole casserole coal dole droll enroll goal hole
loophole Maypole mole Old King Cole oriole parole patrol pole poll
porthole role roll scroll tadpole toll troll whole

convention (see **tension**)

converge (see **verge**)

convince hints mints prince rinse since wince

cook book brook crook hook look mistook nook outlook rook shook
took undertook

cool April fool drool fool ghoul Liverpool overrule pool rule school spool
stool tool whirlpool

cop chop co-opt crop drop eavesdrop flop hip-hop hop lollipop mop plop
pop prop raindrop shop stop swap tip-top whop

copasetic arithmetic arsenic brick candlestick candlewick Catholic chick
click flick heartsick hick kick lick limerick love-sick lunatic maverick
medic nick pick sick slick stick thick tic tick wick

cope antelope cantaloupe dope elope envelope grope gyroscope hope
horoscope kaleidoscope microscope mope pope rope scope slope
soap stethoscope telescope

core (see **door**)

cork fork New York pork torque stork uncork

corn adorn airborne born Cape Horn Capricorn horn lovelorn Matterhorn
morn mourn popcorn scorn stillborn sworn unicorn warn worn

corny horny thorny

correct (see **defect**)

corrupt abrupt cupped disrupt erupt interrupt supped

cost bossed crossed exhaust flossed frost holocaust lost Pentecost tossed

cottage wattage

cotton begotten gotten forgotten rotten

couch crouch grouch ouch pouch slouch vouch

cough off scoff trough

could brotherhood fatherhood firewood good Hollywood hood likelihood
livelihood misunderstood motherhood neighborhood should
sisterhood stood understood withstood womanhood wood would

count account amount dismount fount mount paramount tantamount

couple supple

course coarse divorce endorse force horse Norse reinforce remorse
resource source

court abort assort comfort contort deport distort escort exhort export extort
fort import passport port quart report resort retort short snort sort
sport support thwart tort transport wart

cousin buzzin' cussin' dozen fusin' musin'

cove by Jove clove dove drove grove rove

cover discover hover lover recover rediscover shover undercover (see *her*)

cow allow avow bough bow brow chow disavow endow frau how kowtow
now ow plough plow row slough somehow sow thou vow wow

coy (see **boy**)

CPT (see **be**)

crab blab cab dab drab fab gab grab jab lab nab scab slab stab tab

crabby abbey cabby flabby grabby scabby shabby tabby

crack almanac attack back black Cadillac cardiac clickety-clack crack egomaniac feedback hack Hackensack haystack jack kleptomaniac knack lack mack maniac pack plaque Pontiac Prozac quack rack sack shack slack snack stack tack track whack yak zodiac

craft draft draught graft overdraft witchcraft

crank bank blank clank crank dank drank flank frank Hank jank outrank plank prank rank sank shank shrank skank spank stank tank thank yank

cranky hanky hanky-panky lanky scanky Yankee

craze ablaze amaze appraise bays braze days daze faze gaze glaze graze haze malaise mayonnaise maze nays nowadays plays praise ways

crazy daisy hazy foogazy lazy scrazy

cream beam deem dream esteem extreme gleam ream regime scheme scream seam seen steam stream supreme team teem

creative (see **native**)

creature bleacher feature preacher screecher teacher

cred (see **dead**)

credit accredit discredit edit (see *it*)

crept accept adept except intercept kept overslept slept stepped swept wept

crew (see **do**)

crib ad lib glib rib

cricket picket thicket ticket wicked wicket (see *it*)

crime chime climb dime I'm lime mime pantomime prime rhyme slime show time summertime thyme time

cringe binge fringe hinge infringe singe

crips battleships chips clips dips drips flips grips hips lips quips rips scrips ships slips snips strips tips trips whips

crisp lisp wisp

critic analytic arthritic hypocritic paralytic parasitic Semitic (see *tick*)

critical analytical political

crock (see **clock**)

crocodile (see **smile**)

cronies acrimonies phonies ponies stonys testimonies

Crooklyn aspirin been begin Benjamin Berlin bin chagrin chin discipline feminine fin 5x10 genuine gin grin heroine in inn kin mandolin mannequin masculine moccasin origin pin saccharine shin sin skin spin thick-and-thin thin tin twin violin win within

cross across albatross boss double-cross floss hoss gloss loss moss
rhinoceros sauce toss

crow afro although banjo beau below bestow blow bow buffalo bungalow
calico crossbow depot doe domino dough embryo escrow Eskimo
flow foe forgo fro gazebo gigolo glow go grow heigh-ho ho-ho hobo
hoe incognito indigo Joe know long ago low Mexico mistletoe mow
no oboe oh outgrow overflow overgrow overthrow owe Pinocchio
plateau quo rainbow ratio roe row sew slow snow so Soho status
quo stow studio though throw tiptoe to-and-fro toe Tokyo tow
tremolo undergo undertow vertigo woe yo yo-yo

crowd allowed aloud cloud enshroud loud plowed proud shroud
thundercloud

crown (see **clown**)

crucifix acrobatics bics fiddlesticks fix kicks licks mathematics matrix mix nix
picks politics six sticks Styx ticks transfix tricks wicks

crucifixion addiction affliction benediction contradiction conviction
depiction diction eviction fiction friction jurisdiction prediction
restriction

crude brood clued conclude dude exclude food glued include intrude
misconstrued mood preclude prude rude seclude shrewd wooed

cruel duel fuel jewel

crumb (see **dumb**)

crumble bumble fumble grumble humble jumble mumble rumble
stumble tumble

   crunk bunk chunk clunk cyberpunk drunk dunk flunk funk hunk junk
monk p-funk plunk punk shrunk skunk slunk spunk stunk
sunk trunk

crusade (see **afraid**)

crush blush brush flush gush lush mush plush rush slush thrush underbrush

crutch clutch Dutch hutch inasmuch much retouch such touch

cry alibi amplify banzai barfly butterfly buy by bye certify clarify crucify defy
deify deny die dignify diversify dragonfly drive-by dry dye eye firefly
fly fry FYI glorify gratify guy high horrify I identify imply July justify lie
lullaby modify my mystify notify passerby pie pry qualify rely rye
satisfy sci-fi shy sigh signify simplify sky sly specify spry spy terrify
testify thigh tie try underlie verify why

crypt chipped dipped equipped manuscript script sipped transcript
whipped zipped

crystal pistol

cuba scuba tuba

cube boob rube tube

cucumber cumber encumber lumber number slumber umber

cuddle fuddle huddle muddle puddle

cue (see **knew**)

cuff (see **bluff**)

culture agriculture vulture

cup buttercup fed up hard-up pick-up pup sup up

cupid stupid

curb blurb 'burb disturb herb perturb Serb suburb superb verb

cure allure armature assure brochure caricature cocksure demure endure ensure expenditure forfeiture immature impure insecure insure liqueur literature lure manicure mature miniature obscure overture pedicure premature pure reassure secure signature sure tablature temperature your

curious (see **us**)

curl earl girl hurl pearl swirl twirl whirl

curly burly curly girlie pearly squirrelly surly swirly

curse adverse converse disburse disperse diverse hearse immerse intersperse inverse nurse purse rehearse reverse terse trans-verse traverse universe verse worse

curt (see **hurt**)

curtain blurtin' convertin' desertin' divertin' exertin' flirtin' hurtin' skirtin' squirtin'

curve conserve deserve nerve observe preserve reserve serve swerve

cuss (see **us**)

custody (see **be**)

cut but butt coconut glut gut halibut hut King Tut mutt nut putt rut scuttlebutt shut slut smut strut uncut

cute absolute acute astute attribute beaut boot brute Butte chute commute compute constitute coot destitute dilute dispute disrepute dissolute electrocute en route execute flute fruit hoot loot lute minute moot mute newt parachute persecute pollute prosecute prostitute pursuit recruit refute repute resolute root route scoot shoot snoot substitute suit toot transmute uproot

d

dad (see **mad**)

daddy baddy caddie laddie paddy sugar daddy

dagger carpetbagger stagger swagger

daily Bailey gaily Israeli ukulele

dairy (see **cherry**)

daisy crazy hazy foogazy lazy scrazy

damn (see **am**)

dance advance ants chance circumstance enhance extravagance finance France glance lance pants prance romance stance trance

dandelion buyin' cryin' denyin' dyin' lion lyin' Orion Ryan sighin' tryin' Zion (see *in*)

dang bang boomerang clang fang gang-bang hang orangutan rang sang slang sprang

dangerous (see **us**)

dank (see **drank**)

dap cap chap clap dap flap gap handicap lap map mishap nap rap sap scrap slap snap strap tap trap wrap zap

dapper capper clapper dapper flapper handicapper rapper slapper snapper tapper whippersnapper wiretapper wrapper yapper

dare (see **air**)

dark aardvark arc ark bark embark hark lark mark narc park patriarch remark shark spark stark

dart apart art cart chart counterpart depart heart mart part smart start sweetheart tart upstart

dash ash balderdash bash brash cash clash crash flash gash gnash rash rehash slash smash splash stash thrash trash

date (see **ate**)

daughter blotter hotter otter plotter slaughter spotter squatter trotter water

dawn Amazon Babylon begone bonbon Bonn brawn chiffon con Don drawn fawn gone hexagon John lawn lexicon octagon on Oregon pawn pentagon silicon undergone upon withdrawn wanton yawn

day AK array bay betray blue jay bouquet bray clay decay delay disarray dismay display Dr. Dre eh? essay exposé fray gay gray hay hey holiday hooray José Kay lay matinee may moiré naysay negligée obey parlay pay play portray protégé ray résumé ricochet risqué rosé say slay sleigh soufflé stay stray sway they toupee way veejay weigh word spray x-ray

dead ahead bed bedspread bread bred coed cred dread fed figurehead fled flowerbed fountainhead gingerbread head inbred lead led misled misread overfed read red riverbed said shed shred sled sped spread thoroughbred thread underfed unthread wed

deaf chef clef

deal (see **feel**)

dealer congealer feeler healer reeler sealer squealer stealer wheeler

dear (see **near**)

death breath Macbeth

debate (see **ate**)

debt alphabet bayonet bet brunette cabinet cadet cigarette clarinet cornet corvette duet epithet etiquette forget fret gazette get jet Joliet Juliet let luncheonette marionette met net omelet pet quartet regret roulette set silhouette Somerset sunset sweat threat Tibet toilette upset vet 'vette violet wet yet

decay (see **say**)

decease cease crease decrease fleece geese grease Greece increase lease masterpiece peace piece police release

decent indecent recent

deception conception contraception exception inception perception preconception reception self-deception

decision (see **vision**)

deck check Czech fleck heck neck peck Quebec speck trek wreck

decline (see **fine**)

decoy (see **boy**)

dedicate (see **ate**)

deduct abduct conduct construct instruct obstruct plucked viaduct

deep barkeep cheep creep heap keep leap peep reap seep sheep sleep steep sweep weep

defeat athlete beat beet bittersweet bleat cheat compete complete conceit concrete deceit delete deplete discreet discrete eat elite feat feet fleet greet heat incomplete indiscreet meat meet mistreat neat obsolete parakeet receipt repeat retreat seat sheet sleet street suite sweet treat wheat

defect affect architect bisect checked collect connect correct deflect dialect
direct disinfect dissect effect eject erect expect genuflect incorrect
inject neglect object pecked perfect project prospect protect recollect
reflect reject respect select subject suspect wrecked

defendant ascendant attendant dependent descendant ignorant
independent pendant superintendent transcendent

defender (see **tender**)

defense (see **fence**)

defensive apprehensive comprehensive expensive extensive
incomprehensive inexpensive intensive offensive pensive

defer amateur blur chamber chauffeur concur confer connoisseur demur
deter fur her gangsta incur infer Jennifer myrrh occur per prefer purr
recur sir slur spur stir transfer voyageur were whir

defiance alliance appliance compliance reliance

degree (see **be**)

delay (see **say**)

deli belly celly jelly Kelly Nelly Shelly smelly

delicious (see **vicious**)

delight (see **flight**)

deliver giver liver quiver river shiver sliver (see *her*)

delivery chivalry livery shivery slivery quivery

delo bellow cello fellow hello Jell-o mellow Othello yellow

demand and band brand canned command contraband expand fanned
grand hand land panned planned reprimand Rio Grande sand stand

demo memo

demolish (See **abolish**)

denial dial retrial self-denial trial viol (see *vile*)

dent (see **bent**)

dental (see **gentle**)

deny (see **cry**)

depart apart art cart chart counterpart dart heart mart part smart start
sweetheart tart upstart

depression aggression compression concession confession digression
discretion expression impression indiscretion obsession oppression
possession procession profession progression recession regression
repression secession session succession suppression transgression

deputy (see **be**)

describe bribe circumscribe jibe prescribe scribe subscribe tribe vibe

deserve conserve curve nerve observe preserve reserve serve swerve

desire acquire admire amplifier aspire attire buyer choir conspire crier cryer dire drier dryer entire esquire expire fire flier friar higher hire inquire inspire justifier liar magnifier multiplier mystifier perspire prior prophesier require retire satisfier sire squire supplier testifier tire transpire wire

desk burlesque grotesque picturesque

desperado bravado Colorado El Dorado Laredo Mikado tornado

dessert alert avert blurt concert convert curt curtain desert dirt divert exert expert extrovert flirt hurt insert introvert invert pervert shirt skirt squirt subvert yogurt

destroy (see **boy**)

deviate abbreviate alleviate (see *ate*)

devil bedevil bevel dishevel level revel

diagnosis narcosis neurosis prognosis psychosis

dial denial retrial self-denial trial viol (see *vile*)

diary fiery priory Valkyrie wiry

dice advice concise device entice ice lice mice nice paradise precise price rice sacrifice spice splice suffice thrice twice vice

dictate (see **ate**)

did bid forbid grid hid invalid lid Madrid pyramid rid skid slid squid

die (see **cry**)

died beside bona fide bride collide confide countryside decide defied died dignified divide eyed fireside guide hide hillside homicide inside lied outside override pride provide reside ride side slide snide stride subdivide subside suicide tide tried wide yuletide

diesel easel measle weasel

diet riot quiet (see *it*)

differ sniffer stiffer (see *her*)

difference (see **fence**)

dig big dig fig gig jig pig renege rig swig twig wig underdig

digest (see **best**)

digit fidget midget widget

dignify signify (see *cry*)

dime chime climb crime I'm lime mime pantomime prime rhyme slime show time summertime thyme time

dimension (see **tension**)

dimple pimple simple

dine (see **fine**)

diner cosigner Carolina designer eyeliner finer liner miner minor nina refiner shiner signer

dinner B.F. Skinner beginner breadwinner inner sinner skinner spinner thinner

dinosaur (see **door**)

dip (see **trip**)

diploma aroma coma sarcoma Sonoma Tacoma

direct (see **defect**)

direction (see **affection**)

director collector connector detector deflector injector inspector nectar objector projector prospector protector reflector selector vector (see *her*)

dirt (see **hurt**)

dirty flirty thirty 730

dis abyss amiss analysis armistice bliss carcass cowardice 'dis dismiss emphasis gangstress hiss hypothesis kiss miss mistress nemesis office prejudice Swiss synthesis this

disco Cisco Crisco San Francisco

discuss (see **us**)

disease aborigines appease bees breeze cheese ease expertise freeze Hercules keys knees peas pleas please sees seize Siamese sleaze squeeze tease trapeze zzzs

disgrace ace base bass brace case chase commonplace debase displace embrace encase erase face grace lace mace misplace pace place race replace space steeplechase trace unlace vase

disgust adjust August bust crust distrust dust encrust entrust gust just lust mistrust must robust rust thrust trust unjust

dish devilish fish gibberish impoverish squish swish wish

dismay (see **say**)

distance assistance consistence existence insistence persistence resistance subsistence

distant assistant consistent existent inconsistent insistent persistent resistant subsistent

distaste baste aftertaste braced chaste faced freckle-faced haste hatchet-faced paste taste waist waste

distinction extinction

distort (see **court**)

distortion abortion contortion extortion portion proportion

ditch bewitch bitch ditch enrich glitch hitch pitch rich snitch stitch switch twitch which

divinity (see **be**)

divorce coarse course endorse force horse Norse reinforce remorse resource source

dizzy busy frizzy Lizzie Tin Lizzie tizzy

DNA (see **say**)

do accrue ado bamboo blew blue boo boohoo brew caribou cashew clue construe coo coup crew cuckoo drew flew flue glue gnu goo grew Hindu hitherto hullabaloo igloo impromptu into issue Kalamazoo kangaroo kazoo Kickapoo misconstrue moo outdo overdo overthrew peek-a-boo Peru poo rendezvous screw shampoo shoe shoo shrew Sioux slew slue stew taboo tattoo threw through tissue to too true two undo voodoo wahoo well-to-do who withdrew woo yahoo zoo Zulu (see *you*)

dock (see **clock**)

dodge dislodge hodgepodge lodge

does abuzz buzz cause coz fuzz was

dog analog bog catalog clog cog fog demagogue dialogue epilogue flog frog grog hog jog log monologue synagogue travelogue underdog

dole (see **control**)

dollar bawler brawler call 'er caller choler collar crawler hauler mauler scrawler smaller squalor taller

dolly collie finale folly golly jolly melancholy Molly Polly tamale trolley volley

dolo bolo gigolo piccolo polo rollo solo tremolo

don Amazon autobahn Babylon bonbon Bonn brawn chiffon con Don dawn drawn echelon fawn gone lawn neon on pawn pentagon silicon swan undergone upon wan woebegone wonton yawn

donate (see **ate**)

done anyone begun bun comparison everyone fun Galveston gun hon Hun jettison none nun oblivion one outdone outrun over-done overrun phenomenon pun run shotgun shun simpleton skeleton son stun sun ton unison venison won

doom bloom boom broom cloakroom entomb flume gloom groom room tomb whom womb zoom

door abhor ambassador ashore auditor bachelor Baltimore before boar
bore chancellor chore commodore competitor conspirator
contributor core corps corridor deplore dinosaur drawer Ecuador
editor emperor encore evermore explore exterior floor folklore for
fore four furthermore galore governor ignore implore inferior lore
matador metaphor more nevermore nor oar offshore or orator ore
poor pour rapport restore roar score seashore senator señor shore
Singapore snore soar sophomore sore spore store swore therefore
Thor tore troubadour underscore uproar visitor whore yore your

dope antelope cantaloupe cope elope envelope grope gyroscope hope
horoscope kaleidoscope microscope mope pope rope scope slope
soap stethoscope telescope

do-rag bag brag drag flag gag hag lag mag nag rag sag shag slag snag stag
swag tag wag

dose adios bellicose close comatose diagnose engross grandiose gross
morose nose overdose varicose verbose

double bubble rubble stubble trouble

doubt about boy scout blow-out bout clout devout flout gout lout out pout
roundabout route scout shout snout spout sprout stout tout trout
wash-out worn-out

dough afro although banjo beau below bestow blow bow buffalo bungalow
calico crossbow crow depot doe domino dough embryo escrow
Eskimo flow foe forgo fro gazebo gigolo glow go grow heigh-ho ho-
ho hobo hoe incognito indigo Joe know long ago low Mexico
mistletoe mow no oboe oh outgrow overflow overgrow overthrow
owe Pinocchio plateau quo rainbow ratio roe row sew slow snow so
Soho status quo stow studio though throw tiptoe to-and-fro toe
Tokyo tow tremolo undergo undertow vertigo woe yo yo-yo

dove above glove ladylove love mourning dove of shove turtle dove

dove by Jove clove cove drove grove rove

down brown clown crown downtown drown frown gown hand-me-down lock-
down noun Oaktown renown town tumble-down upside down uptown

dozen buzzin' cousin cussin' fusin' musin'

Dr. Dre (see **say**)

draft craft draught graft overdraft witchcraft

drafted grafted shafted (see *did*)

drag bag brag do-rag flag gag hag lag mag nag rag sag shag slag snag stag
swag tag wag

drama Bahama comma Dalai Lama llama mamma melodrama pajama Yokohama

drank bank blank clank crank dank flank frank Hank jank outrank plank prank rank sank shank shrank skank spank stank tank thank yank

drastic bombastic elastic enthusiastic fantastic gymnastic iconoclastic plastic sarcastic scholastic spastic

draw Arkansas awe bra caw claw flaw gnaw guffaw hurrah jaw law Ma nah outlaw overdraw Pa paw raw saw seesaw shah slaw squaw straw thaw withdraw

drawn (see **dawn**)

dread (see **said**)

dreadlocks boondocks clocks cocks cornstalks crocks deadlocks defrocks docks flintlocks flocks frocks glocks gridlocks hawks hocks knocks locks mocks Mohawks padlocks peacocks rocks shocks socks squawks stalks stocks tomahawks unlocks

dream beam cream deem esteem extreme gleam ream regime scheme scream seam seen steam stream supreme team teem

dreamt attempt contempt exempt tempt unkempt

dreamy creamy seamy steamy (see *me*)

dress (see **confess**)

dressy messy

drew (see **do**)

drift gift lift shift spendthrift swift thrift

drill (see **fill**)

drink blink brink chink clink fink hoodwink ink kink link mink pink rink shrink sink slink stink wink zinc

drizzle chisel fizzle frizzle grizzle sizzle swizzle

drop chop co-opt cop crop eavesdrop flop hip-hop hop lollipop mop plop pop prop raindrop shop stop swap tip-top whop

drove by Jove clove cove dove grove rove

drug bug dug jug hug lug mug plug pug rug shrug slug smug snug thug tug

drum (see **dumb**)

drummer comer dumber hummer newcomer strummer summer

drunk bunk chunk clunk crunk cyberpunk dunk flunk funk hunk junk monk p-funk plunk punk shrunk skunk slunk spunk stunk sunk trunk

drunken shrunken sunken

dry alibi amplify banzai barfly butterfly buy by bye certify clarify crucify cry defy deify deny die dignify diversify dragonfly drive-by dye eye firefly

fly fry FYI glorify gratify guy high horrify I identify imply July justify lie lullaby modify my mystify notify passerby pie pry qualify rely rye satisfy sci-fi shy sigh signify simplify sky sly specify spry spy terrify testify thigh tie try underlie verify why

duce (see **abuse**)

duck (see **truck**)

dude (see **feud, mood**)

due (see **knew**)

duel cruel fuel jewel perusal renewal

dug bug drug jug hug lug mug plug pug rug shrug slug smug snug thug tug

duke juke puke uke

dull annul cull gull hull lull mull scull skull

dumb album aquarium auditorium become bum burdensome Christendom come cranium crematorium crumb curriculum drum emporium fee-fi-fo-fum glum gum gymnasium hum kettledrum kingdom martyrdom maximum meddlesome medium millennium minimum mum museum numb opium overcome pendulum petroleum platinum plum premium quarrelsome radium random rum sanitarium scum slum some strum succumb sum swum tedium thumb Tom Thumb Tweedledum uranium worrisome yum

dummy crummy gummy mummy rummy tummy yummy

dump bump chump clump hump jump lump plump rump slump stump thump trump ump

dupe coop droop group hoop loop nincompoop poop scoop sloop soup stoop swoop troop troupe whoop

duplex BMX complex decks DMX ex flex hex Lex necks pecks reflex Rolodex sex specs Tex unisex

during alluring assuring blurring concurring conferring curing deferring demurring deterring enduring ensuring incurring inferring insuring interring luring maturing occurring preferring procuring purring referring securing spurring transferring whirring

dusk husk musk tusk

dust adjust August bust crust dust disgust distrust encrust entrust gust just lust mistrust must robust rust thrust trust unjust

duty beauty cutie patootie

dwarf wharf

dwindle kindle rekindle spindle swindle

dynamic ceramic Islamic panoramic

e

each beach breach impeach leech peach preach reach screech
speech teach

eager beleaguer intriguer leaguer meager overeager

eagle beagle illegal legal regal sea gull

ear adhere appear atmosphere auctioneer beer bombardier career cashier
cavalier chandelier cheer clear dear deer disappear engineer fear
financier frontier gear hear hemisphere here insincere interfere jeer
lavaliere leer mere mountaineer near overhear overseer peer
persevere pioneer queer racketeer reappear rear revere seer severe
shear sheer sincere smear sneer spear sphere stratosphere tear
veneer volunteer year

earl curl earl girl hurl pearl swirl twirl whirl

earn adjourn burn churn concern discern fern intern kern learn overturn
return sojourn spurn stern taciturn turn urn yearn

earth birth dearth girth mirth worth

ease aborigines appease bees breeze cheese disease expertise freeze
Hercules keys knees peas pleas please sees seize Siamese sleaze
squeeze tease trapeze zzzs

easel diesel measle weasel

east beast ceased creased deceased feast least pieced priest yeast

easy breezy cheesy greasy queasy sleazy sneezy speakeasy wheezy

eat athlete beat beet bittersweet bleat cheat compete complete conceit
concrete deceit defeat delete deplete discreet discrete elite feat feet
fleet greet heat incomplete indiscreet meat meet mistreat neat
obsolete parakeet receipt repeat retreat seat sheet sleet street suite
sweet treat wheat

ebony (see **be**)

e-box box chickenpox equinox fox mailbox orthodox ox paradox

echo art deco deco gecko (see *glow*)

ecstasy (see **be**)

Eden leadin' needin' readin' seedin' Sweden weedin'

edge allege dredge fledge hedge ledge privilege sacrilege sledge wedge

educate (see **ate**)

effect affect architect bisect checked collect connect correct defect deflect
dialect direct disinfect dissect eject erect expect genuflect incorrect

inject neglect object pecked perfect project prospect protect recollect reflect reject respect select subject suspect wrecked

either breather neither

elapse caps collapse craps flaps lapse maps naps perhaps saps traps wraps

elbow (see **flow**)

election (see **affection**)

elf herself himself itself myself self shelf yourself

elm helm realm overwhelm whelm

elope (see **hope**)

embargo argot cargo Fargo largo

embrace ace base bass brace case chase commonplace debase disgrace displace encase erase face grace lace mace misplace pace place race replace space steeplechase trace unlace vase

emerge (see **verge**)

Eminem Bethlehem brim condemn dim gem grim gym him hymn limb pseudonym skim slim stem swim them trim whim

emotion commotion locomotion lotion motion notion ocean potion promotion

emperor (see **door**)

enchant (see **ant**)

encore (see **door**)

end apprehend ascend attend befriend bend blend commend comprehend condescend defend depend descend dividend expend extend fend friend intend lend mend offend penned pretend recommend send spend suspend tend transcend trend unbend

ended amended apprehended ascended attended befriended bended blended commended comprehended condescended contended defended depended descended expended extended fended intended mended misapprehended offended portended pretended recommended splendid suspended tended unattended unblended

endurance assurance insurance

endure (see **cure**)

enemy (see **be**)

energy (see **be**)

enjoy annoy boy convoy corduroy coy decoy destroy employ homeboy Illinois joy ploy Roy Savoy soy toy troy

enough bluff buff cuff duff fluff gruff huff muff powder puff rough scruff
    scuff snuff stuff tough

enter center dissenter experimenter frequenter inventor mentor presenter
    preventer renter tormenter

envelope (see **hope**)

episode (see **road**)

equation abrasion dissuasion evasion invasion occasion persuasion

erase (see **embrace**)

erect (see **effect**)

erotic chaotic exotic hypnotic idiotic macrobiotic narcotic neurotic quixotic

erratic (see **attic**)

error bearer carer darer terror wearer

erupt abrupt corrupt cupped disrupt interrupt supped

escape ape cape cityscape drape grape landscape rape seascape
    shape tape

essence adolescence convalescence fluorescence incandescence
    obsolescence

esteem beam cream deem dream extreme gleam ream regime scheme
    scream seam seen steam stream supreme team teem

eternal colonel external fraternal infernal internal journal kernel maternal
    nocturnal paternal

eternity fraternity maternity paternity

European Caribbean Crimean Galilean peon (see *in*)

Evangelist (see **exist**)

evasive dissuasive invasive persuasive pervasive

eve achieve believe bereave conceive disbelieve grieve heave leave
    perceive receive relieve reprieve retrieve sleeve weave

evening (see **sing**)

event (see *bent*)

eventful resentful

everyone anyone begun bun comparison done fun Galveston gun hon
    Hun jettison none nun oblivion one outdone outrun over-done
    overrun phenomenon pun run shotgun shun simpleton skeleton son
    stun sun ton unison venison won

everything (see **sing**)

evict addict conflict constrict contradict convict derelict flicked inflict licked
    predict pricked strict

evil medieval primeval upheaval weevil
evolution (see **revolution**)
ex BMX complex decks DMX duplex flex hex Lex necks pecks reflex Rolodex
sex specs Tex unisex
exact (see **act**)
examine famine
example ample sample trample
except accept adept crept intercept kept overslept slept stepped swept wept
exception conception contraception deception inception perception
preconception reception self-deception
excite appetite bite blight bright byte contrite copyright daylight delight
despite dynamite Fahrenheit fight flight fright head-light height ignite
invite kite knight light midnight might moonlight night outright
parasite plight polite quite recite reunite right satellite sight site
sleight slight spite starlight sunlight tight trite twilight unite white write
excuse abuse accuse confuse cues deduce diffuse disuse duce induce
infuse introduce juice misuse obtuse peruse produce profuse reduce
refuse reproduce seduce Syracuse use
execution (see **revolution**)
exhibit inhibit prohibit
exist accompanist analyst anarchist anthropologist archeologist assist
biologist Calvinist capitalist coexist communist consist cyst desist
dismissed egoist essayist evangelist exorcist fatalist gist hissed
humanist humorist idealist imperialist insist journalist kissed list
lobbyist Methodist missed mist moralist motorist nationalist novelist
organist perfectionist pharmacist pianist plagiarist psychologist
romanticist satirist sentimentalist socialist soloist specialist strategist
terrorist theologist theorist twist ventriloquist vocalist wordsmith wrist
existed (see **twisted**)
exotic chaotic erotic hypnotic idiotic macrobiotic narcotic neurotic quixotic
expect (see **effect**)
expense (see **fence**)
expensive apprehensive comprehensive defensive extensive
incomprehensive inexpensive intensive offensive pensive
expert (see **hurt**)
explain abstain again airplane arraign ascertain attain brain Cain campaign
cane chain champagne cocaine complain contain crane detain
disdain domain drain entertain feign gain grain humane hurricane

hydroplane insane lane main Maine maintain mane migraine obtain ordain pain pane pertain plain plane profane propane rain refrain reign rein remain sane slain Spain sprain stain strain sustain train vain vane vein wane windowpane

explode (see **road**)

explore (see **door**)

export (see **court**)

exposure closure composure disclosure foreclosure

exterior inferior interior superior ulterior

extinction distinction

extortion abortion contortion extortion portion proportion

extreme beam cream deem dream esteem gleam ream regime scheme scream seam seen steam stream supreme team teem

extra abc-ya duh Oprah extra zebra (see *raw*)

eye alibi amplify banzai barfly buy by bye certify clarify crucify cry defy deify deny die dignify diversify dragonfly drive-by dry dye firefly fly fry FYI glorify gratify guy high horrify I identify imply July justify lie lullaby modify my mystify notify passerby pie pry qualify rely rye satisfy sci-fi shy sigh signify simplify sky sly specify spry spy terrify testify thigh tie try underlie verify why

eyes (see **lies**)

F

fab blab cab crab dab drab fab gab grab jab lab nab scab slab stab tab
fable (see **able**)
face ace base bass brace case chase commonplace debase disgrace
　　　　displace embrace encase erase grace lace mace misplace pace
　　　　place race replace space steeplechase trace unlace vase
facial glacial racial spatial
fact (see **act**)
factor actor benefactor contractor detractor distracter extractor raptor reactor
　　　　refractor tractor
factory refractory satisfactory (see *story, be*)
factual actual contractual
fade (see **afraid**)
fail ale bail bale blackmail Braille cocktail curtail exhale female flail frail hail
　　　　hale impale inhale jail mail male nail pale prevail rail regale sail sale
　　　　scale shale snail stale tail they'll veil whale
faint acquaint ain't complaint paint quaint restraint saint taint 'tain't
fair (see **air**)
fairy (see **cherry**)
fake ache bake brake break cake flake forsake headache heartache
　　　　keepsake make mistake opaque quake rake sake shake snake stake
　　　　steak take wake
fall all ball bawl brawl call crawl doll drawl gall haul install mall maul
　　　　Montreal nightfall overhaul parasol pitfall protocol rainfall scrawl
　　　　shawl small snowfall sprawl stall tall thrall wall waterfall y'all
fam am Amsterdam anagram Birmingham cam clam cram dam damn
　　　　diaphragm gram ham jam lamb ma'am madame scram sham slam
　　　　swam telegram tram yam
fame acclaim aim became blame came claim exclaim flame frame game
　　　　inflame lame maim name proclaim same shame tame
family (see **be**)
famine examine
famous (see **us**)
fantastic bombastic drastic elastic enthusiastic gymnastic iconoclastic
　　　　plastic sarcastic scholastic spastic
fantasy (see **be**)

far A&R are bar bazaar bizarre car caviar cigar czar disbar guitar jar par radar scar sitar spar star tar

farce parse sparse

farm arm alarm charm disarm forearm harm

fashion ashen bashin' compassion impassion passion

fast aghast blast cast classed contrast flabbergast forecast gassed last mast outlast overcast passed past vast

fat (see **at**)

F

fatigue intrigue league

fatty batty catty chatty Cincinnati natty Patty ratty

fault assault cobalt exalt halt malt salt somersault vault

favor braver cadaver favor flavor graver paver saver savor shaver waiver waver

fear adhere appear atmosphere auctioneer beer bombardier career cashier cavalier chandelier cheer clear dear deer disappear ear engineer financier frontier gear hear hemisphere here insincere interfere jeer lavaliere leer mere mountaineer near overhear overseer peer persevere pioneer queer racketeer reappear rear revere seer severe shear sheer sincere smear sneer spear sphere stratosphere tear veneer volunteer year

feast beast ceased creased deceased east least pieced priest yeast

feat (see **sweet**)

feather altogether Heather leather tether together weather whether (see *her*)

feature bleacher creature preacher screecher teacher

fed ahead bed bedspread bread bred coed dead dread figurehead fled flowerbed fountainhead gingerbread head inbred lead led misled misread overfed read red riverbed said shed shred sled sped spread thoroughbred thread underfed unthread wed

fee (see **be**)

feed agreed bleed breed centipede concede creed deed exceed greed heed inbreed knead lead mislead need precede proceed read recede reed secede seed speed stampede succeed Swede tweed weed

feel appeal automobile Bastille Camille conceal deal eel genteel he'll heal heel ideal kneel meal mobile peel real reel repeal reveal seal she'll spiel squeal steal steel veal we'll wheal zeal

feeling appealing ceiling concealing congealing dealing healing kneeling pealing peeling reeling repealing revealing squealing stealing unfeeling wheeling

feet (see **sweet**)

feline beeline sea-line (see *mine*)

fell bell belle Carmel carrousel cell clientele dell dwell excel farewell gel hell hotel infidel knell mademoiselle personnel sell shell smell spell tell well yell

fellow bellow cello delo hello Jell-o mellow Othello yellow

felt belt Celt dealt heartfelt melt pelt welt

female (see **fail**)

feminine (see **been**)

fence abstinence affluence benevolence circumference coincidence commence competence condense conference confidence consequence convenience defense difference dispense dissidence eloquence evidence excellence expense experience frankincense immense impotence incense incidence incompetence indigence influence innocence intense magnificence negligence obedience permanence preference pretense reference reverence sense suspense tense violence

fern (see **learn**)

fertile girdle hurdle myrtle turtle

fetch catch etch kvetch retch sketch stretch wretch

fetti confetti fetti jetty machete petty spaghetti sweaty

feud allude altitude aptitude attitude delude dude fortitude gratitude interlude latitude lewd longitude magnitude multitude nude prelude pursued renewed solitude subdued sued 'tude you'd

fever achiever beaver believer cleaver deceiver leave 'er receiver reliever retriever weaver

few (see **knew**)

fib ad lib crib glib rib

fiction addiction affliction benediction contradiction conviction crucifixion depiction diction eviction friction jurisdiction prediction restriction

fiddle diddle griddle middle riddle twiddle

field battlefield Chesterfield shield wield yield

fiend cleaned gleaned meaned quarantined weaned

fierce pierce

fiery (see **be**)

fight (see **flight**)

figment pigment

file aisle awhile beguile bile compile crocodile defile isle juvenile meanwhile mile Nile pile rile smile style tile vile while wile worthwhile

fill bill chill daffodil distill drill frill fulfill gill grill hill ill imbecile instill kill mill nil quill shrill sill skill spill still swill thrill till trill until whippoorwill will windmill windowsill

final spinal vinyl

finance advance ants chance circumstance dance enhance extravagance France glance lance pants prance romance stance trance

fine align asinine assign benign combine concubine confine consign decline define design dine divine entwine incline line malign mine nine outshine pine porcupine recline refine resign Rhine shine shrine sign spine stein swine twine underline undermine vine whine wine

finger linger (see *her*)

finish diminish Finnish

fire acquire admire amplifier aspire attire buyer choir conspire crier cryer desire dire drier dryer entire esquire expire flier friar higher hire inquire inspire justifier liar magnifier multiplier mystifier perspire prior prophesier require retire satisfier sire squire supplier testifier tire transpire wire

firm affirm confirm germ reaffirm sperm squirm term worm

first burst cursed nursed outburst thirst versed worst

fish devilish dish gibberish impoverish squish swish wish

fit befit bit 'git grit kit knit hit it jit legit lit nit-wit pit quit sit spit twit unfit wit zit

five by ten (5x10) aspirin been begin Benjamin Berlin bin chagrin chin Crooklyn discipline feminine fin genuine gin grin heroine in inn kin mandolin mannequin masculine moccasin origin pin saccharine shin sin skin spin thick-and-thin thin tin twin violin win within

fix acrobatics bics crucifix fiddlesticks kicks licks mathematics matrix mix nix picks politics six sticks Styx ticks transfix tricks wicks

fixture mixture

fizz biz frizz his is quiz showbiz 'tis whiz

fizzle chisel drizzle frizzle grizzle sizzle swizzle

flag bag brag drag gag hag lag mag nag rag sag shag slag snag stag swag tag wag

flame acclaim aim became blame came claim exclaim fame frame game inflame lame maim name proclaim same shame tame

flannel channel panel

flap cap chap clap dap flap gap handicap lap map mishap nap rap sap
  scrap slap snap strap tap trap wrap zap

flares affairs airs billionaires cares chairs compares dares declares despairs
  fairs glares hairs heirs impairs legionnaires millionaires nightmares
  pairs pears prayers prepares repairs scares snares spares squares
  stairs stares swears tears thoroughfares

flash ash balderdash bash brash cash clash crash dash gash gnash rash
  rehash slash smash splash stash thrash trash

F

flat (see **at**)

flattery battery (see *be*)

flaunt daunt gaunt haunt jaunt taunt want

flea (see **be**)

flesh enmesh fresh mesh refresh

flew (see **do**)

flick (see **kick**)

flight appetite bite blight bright byte contrite copyright daylight delight
  despite dynamite excite Fahrenheit fight fright head-light height ignite
  invite kite knight light midnight might moonlight night outright
  parasite plight polite quite recite reunite right satellite sight site
  sleight slight spite starlight sunlight tight trite twilight unite white write

flip battleship chip clip dip drip equip grip gyp hip lip nip quip rip scrip ship
  slip snip strip tip trip whip zip

flirt alert avert blurt concert convert curt curtain desert dessert dirt divert
  exert expert extrovert insert introvert invert pervert shirt skirt squirt
  subvert yogurt

float (see **boat**)

flock (see **clock**)

flood blood bud cud dud mud scud spud stud thud

floor abhor ambassador ashore auditor bachelor Baltimore before boar
  bore chancellor chore commodore competitor conspirator
  contributor core corps corridor deplore dinosaur door drawer
  Ecuador editor emperor encore evermore explore exterior folklore for
  fore four furthermore galore governor ignore implore inferior lore
  matador metaphor more nevermore nor oar offshore or orator ore
  poor pour rapport restore roar score seashore senator señor shore
  Singapore snore soar sophomore sore spore store swore therefore
  Thor tore troubadour underscore uproar visitor whore yore your

flop (see **drop**)

flourish amateurish nourish

flow afro although banjo beau below bestow blow bow buffalo
bungalow calico crossbow crow depot doe domino dough
embryo escrow Eskimo foe forgo fro gazebo gigolo glow go grow
heigh-ho ho-ho hobo hoe incognito indigo Joe know long ago
low Mexico mistletoe mow no oboe oh outgrow overflow
overgrow overthrow owe Pinocchio plateau quo rainbow ratio roe
row sew slow snow so Soho status quo stow studio though
throw tiptoe to-and-fro toe Tokyo tow tremolo undergo undertow
vertigo woe yo yo-yo

flower cauliflower cower deflower empower horsepower plower power
shower tower (see *our*)

flowery bowery dowry floury flowery showery

flowing blowing bowing crowing glowing going growing hoeing knowing
mowing overflowing owing rowing sewing showing slowing snowing
sowing stowing throwing towing

flown (see **known**)

fluffy huffy puffy stuffy

fluke kook spook

flunk bunk chunk clunk crunk cyberpunk drunk dunk funk hunk junk monk
p-funk plunk punk shrunk skunk slunk spunk stunk sunk trunk

flute (see **cute**)

fly alibi amplify banzai barfly butterfly buy by bye certify clarify crucify cry
defy deify deny die dignify diversify dragonfly drive-by dry dye eye
firefly fry FYI glorify gratify guy high horrify I identify imply July justify
lie lullaby modify my mystify notify passerby pie pry qualify rely rye
satisfy sci-fi shy sigh signify simplify sky sly specify spry spy terrify
testify thigh tie try underlie verify why

focus hocus-pocus locus (see *us*)

foe (see **blow**)

fog analog bog catalog clog cog demagogue dialogue dog epilogue
flog frog grog hog hot dog jog log monologue prairie dog
synagogue travelogue

foggy doggy froggy groggy soggy

foil broil coil loyal oil recoil royal spoil toil turmoil

fold behold blindfold bold centerfold cold foothold foretold gold hold
household marigold mold old retold scold sold told uphold withhold

folk (see **joke**)

follow Apollo hollow swallow wallow

folly collie dolly finale golly jolly melancholy Molly Polly tamale trolley volley

fond beyond blond bond correspond dawned pond respond spawned
vagabond wand yawned

food brood clued conclude crude dude exclude glued include intrude
misconstrued mood preclude prude rude seclude shrewd wooed

foogazy crazy daisy hazy lazy scrazy

fool April fool cool drool ghoul Liverpool overrule pool rule school spool
stool tool whirlpool

foot afoot lead foot pussyfoot tenderfoot put

for (see **door**)

forbid bid did grid hid invalid lid Madrid pyramid rid skid slid squid

Ford (see **lord**)

foreclosure closure composure disclosure exposure

forever clever endeavor ever however lever never sever whatever
whenever wherever whoever

forge George gorge

forget alphabet bayonet bet brunette cabinet cadet cigarette clarinet cornet
corvette debt duet epithet etiquette fret gazette get jet Joliet Juliet let
luncheonette marionette met net omelet pet quartet regret roulette
set silhouette Somerset sunset sweat threat Tibet toilette upset vet
'vette violet wet yet

forgiven driven given (see *in*)

forgotten begotten cotton gotten rotten

fork cork New York pork torque stork uncork

form chloroform conform deform inform norm perform rainstorm reform
snowstorm storm swarm transform uniform warm

formal abnormal informal normal

fort (see **court**)

forth fourth henceforth north

forty (see **be**)

fossil apostle colossal docile jostle

fought astronaut bought brought caught cosmonaut fought naught ought
overwrought sought taught thought wrought

foul cowl foul growl howl jowl owl prowl scowl waterfowl

found abound around astound background battleground bloodhound
bound compound confound downed dumbfound ground hound

impound merry-go-round mound pound profound renowned resound round sound spellbound surround under-ground wound

foundry boundary

fox box chickenpox e-box equinox mailbox orthodox ox paradox

fragile agile (see *smile, fill*)

fragrance flagrance vagrants

frantic antic Atlantic chromatic gigantic pedantic romantic transatlantic

fraternity eternity maternity paternity

F

fraud abroad applaud awed broad clod cod defraud façade God guffawed Izod nod odd pod prod promenade quad rod roughshod shod sod squad trod wad

freak beak bleak creek eek geek leak meek reek seek speak tweak weak week

freckle heckle speckle

freeze (see **ease**)

fresh enmesh flesh mesh refresh

friction affliction benediction contradiction conviction crucifixion depiction diction eviction fiction jurisdiction prediction restriction

friend apprehend ascend attend befriend bend blend commend comprehend condescend defend depend descend dividend end expend extend fend intend lend mend offend penned pretend recommend send spend suspend tend transcend trend unbend

fright (see **flight**)

frigid rigid

fringe binge cringe hinge infringe singe

frisky risky whiskey

frog analog bog catalog clog cog fog demagogue dialogue dog epilogue frog grog hog jog log monologue synagogue travelogue

front affront blunt brunt bunt confront forefront grunt hunt punt runt shunt stunt

frost bossed cost crossed exhaust flossed holocaust lost Pentecost tossed

frown brown clown crown down downtown drown frown gown hand-me-down lock-down noun Oaktown renown town tumble-down upside down uptown

froze arose chose close compose decompose depose disclose dispose doze enclose expose foreclose goes hose impose indispose knows nose owes pose predispose presuppose prose rose suppose those toes transpose woes

frozen chosen dozin' mosin' nosin' posin'
fruit (see **cute**)
frustrate (see **ate**)
fry (see **cry**)
fuel cruel duel jewel duel perusal renewal
fun anyone begun bun comparison done everyone Galveston gun hon Hun
jettison none nun oblivion one outdone outrun over-done overrun
phenomenon pun run shotgun shun simpleton skeleton son stun
sun ton unison venison won

function conjunction junction injunction
fund cummerbund refund rotund shunned
funky chunky flunky monkey spunky
funny bunny honey sunny
fur (see **her**)
fury curry flurry hurry jury Missouri scurry slurry surrey worry
fuss (see **us**)
future suture
fuzz abuzz buzz cause coz does was
FYI alibi amplify banzai barfly butterfly buy by bye certify clarify crucify defy
deify deny die dignify diversify dragonfly drive-by dry dye eye firefly
fly fry glorify gratify guy high horrify I identify imply July justify lie
lullaby modify my mystify notify passerby pie pry qualify rely rye
satisfy sci-fi shy sigh signify simplify sky sly specify spry spy terrify
testify thigh tie try underlie verify why

> Most disc jockeys at parties would simply
> play a record all the way to the end, but
> I was too fidgety to just wait for the end
> of the record. So rather than sit and
> wait, I would do something to enhance
> the music.
>
> —Grandmaster Flash

g (see **be**)

gag bag brag drag flag hag lag mag nag rag sag shag slag snag stag swag tag wag

gain abstain again airplane arraign ascertain attain brain Cain campaign cane chain champagne cocaine complain contain crane detain disdain domain drain entertain explain feign grain humane hurricane hydroplane insane lane main Maine maintain mane migraine obtain ordain pain pane pertain plain plane profane propane rain refrain reign rein remain sane slain Spain sprain stain strain sustain train vain vane vein wane windowpane

gal canal chorale morale pal shall

galaxy (see **be**)

gallery calorie Mallory salary

gamble amble ramble scramble shamble

gang-bangin' boomerangin' clangin' hangin' slangin' sprangin'

gangsta amateur chauffeur concur defer demur deter fur her occur purr recur sir slur spur stir transfer voyageur were

gangstress abyss amiss analysis armistice bliss carcass cowardice dis dismiss emphasis gangstress hiss hypothesis kiss miss mistress nemesis office prejudice Swiss synthesis this

gank bank blank clank crank dank drank flank frank gank Hank jank outrank plank prank rank sank shank shrank skank spank stank tank thank yank

garage barrage camouflage entourage mirage

garden harden pardon

gash ash balderdash bash brash cash clash crash dash flash gnash lash rash rehash slash smash splash stash thrash trash

gasoline (see **mean**)

gasp asp clasp grasp

gat at acrobat aristocrat autocrat bat brat bureaucrat cat chat democrat diplomat drat fat flat gnat hat mat pat phat rat rat-a-tat-tat sat scat spat stat thermostat vat

gave behave brave cave concave crave engrave forgave grave knave pave rave save shave slave waive wave

gavel gravel ravel travel unravel

gawk (see **clock**)

gaze ablaze amaze appraise bays blaze braze craze days daze faze glaze graze
       haze malaise mayonnaise maze nays nowadays plays praise ways

geek beak bleak creek eek freak geek leak meek reek seek speak tweak
       weak week

geese cease crease decease decrease fleece grease Greece increase lease
        masterpiece peace piece police release

gem Bethlehem condemn Eminem hem phlegm requiem stem them

gender (see **tender**)

generic atmospheric cleric Derrick esoteric hemispheric hysteric numeric

gentle accidental coincidental complemental compliment continental
         dental departmental detrimental experimental fundamental
         governmental incidental intercontinental lentil mental monumental
         Oriental parental regimental rental rudimental sentimental
         supplemental temperamental

gently evidently impotently innocently insolently intently

germ affirm confirm firm reaffirm sperm squirm term worm

get alphabet bayonet bet brunette cabinet cadet cigarette clarinet cornet
      corvette debt duet epithet etiquette forget fret gazette jet Joliet Juliet
      let luncheonette marionette met net omelet pet quartet regret
      roulette set silhouette Somerset sunset sweat threat Tibet toilette
      upset vet 'vette violet wet yet

g-four (see **door**)

g-funk (see **junk**)

ghetto afro although amoretto banjo beau below bestow blow bow buffalo
         bungalow calico crossbow crow depot doe domino dough embryo
         escrow Eskimo flow foe forgo fro gazebo gigolo go grow heigh ho
         ho-ho hobo hoe incognito indigo Joe know long-ago low Mexico
         mistletoe mow no oboe oh outgrow overflow overgrow overthrow
         owe Pinocchio plateau quo rainbow ratio roe row sew slow snow so
         Soho status stiletto quo stow studio though throw tiptoe to-and-fro
         toe Tokyo tow tremolo undergo undertow vertigo woe yo yo-yo

ghost boast coast foremost furthermost host innermost most post roast
        toast whipping post

giant client compliant defiant reliant self-reliant

gift drift lift shift spendthrift swift thrift

giggle jiggle squiggle wiggle wriggle

gigolo bolo dolo piccolo polo rollo solo tremolo

gin aspirin been begin Benjamin Berlin bin chagrin chin Crooklyn discipline feminine fin 5x10 genuine grin heroine in inn kin mandolin mannequin masculine moccasin origin pin saccharine shin sin skin spin thick-and-thin thin tin twin violin win within

girl curl earl hurl pearl swirl twirl whirl

give affirmative alternative argumentative combative competitive consecutive conservative definitive expletive figurative forgive fugitive informative intuitive live lucrative narrative negative positive primitive prohibitive provocative relative representative sensitive talkative tentative

glad ad add bad Brad cad Chad clad Dad egad fad grad had lad mad nomad pad plaid sad shad Trinidad

glamorous amorous clamorous (see *us*)

glamour clamor damn 'er grammar hammer slammer sledgehammer stammer yammer

glance advance ants chance circumstance dance enhance extravagance finance France lance pants prance romance stance trance

glass (see **class**)

glitter bitter counterfeiter critter fitter fritter litter quitter sitter transmitter twitter (see *her*)

gloat (see **boat**)

globe disrobe Job probe robe strobe

glock Bangkok beanstalk boondock clock cock cornstalk crock deadlock defrock dock dreadlock flintlock flock frock gawk glock gridlock hawk hock jock knock Little Rock livestock lock mock Mohawk padlock peacock rock shock sidewalk Tupoc smock sock squawk stalk stock talk tomahawk unlock walk wok

gloom bloom boom broom cloakroom doom entomb flume groom room tomb whom womb zoom

glorify alibi amplify banzai barfly butterfly buy by bye certify clarify crucify defy deify deny die dignify diversify dragonfly drive-by dry dye eye firefly fly fry FYI glorify gratify guy high horrify I identify imply July justify lie lullaby modify my mystify notify passerby pie pry qualify rely rye satisfy sci-fi shy sigh signify simplify sky sly specify spry spy terrify testify thigh tie try underlie verify why

glory accusatory allegory category dormitory dory gory hunky-dory laboratory Lori obligatory observatory oratory Peter Lorre quarry reformatory retaliatory sorry story territory Tory

9

glove above dove ladylove love mourning dove of shove turtle dove
glow (see **go**)
glue (see **do**)
glum (see **numb**)
glut (see **but**)
g-money bunny funny honey money sunny
go afro although banjo beau below bestow blow bow buffalo bungalow calico crossbow crow depot doe domino dough embryo escrow Eskimo flow foe forgo fro gazebo ghetto gigolo glow grow heigh ho ho-ho hobo hoe incognito indigo Joe know long-ago low Mexico mistletoe mow no oboe oh outgrow overflow overgrow overthrow owe Pinocchio plateau quo rainbow ratio roe row sew slow snow so Soho status quo stow studio though throw tiptoe to-and-fro toe Tokyo tow tremolo undergo undertow vertigo woe yo yo-yo
goal (see **hole**)
god abroad applaud awed broad clod cod defraud façade fraud guffawed Izod nod odd pod prod promenade quad rod roughshod shod sod squad trod wad
goggle boggle boondoggle toggle
gold behold blindfold bold centerfold cold fold foothold foretold hold household marigold mold old retold scold sold told uphold withhold
golly collie dolly finale folly jolly melancholy Molly Polly tamale trolley volley
gone Amazon autobahn Babylon bonbon Bonn brawn chiffon con Don dawn drawn echelon fawn lawn neon on pawn pentagon silicon swan undergone upon wan woebegone wonton yawn
good brotherhood could fatherhood firewood Hollyhood Hollywood hood likelihood livelihood misunderstood motherhood neighborhood should sisterhood stood understood withstood womanhood wood would
goose ace-deuce caboose juice loose moose noose papoose recluse spruce truce vamoose
gorilla guerrilla Manila Priscilla vanilla villa
gory (see **story**)
gown (see **clown**)
GP (see **be**)
grab blab cab crab dab drab fab gab jab lab nab scab slab stab tab
grace ace base bass brace case chase commonplace debase disgrace

displace embrace encase erase face lace mace misplace pace place race replace space steeplechase trace unlace vase

grade aid arcade afraid barricade blade blockade braid brayed brigade charade crusade degrade dismayed dissuade downgrade escapade evade fade grenade hayed invade laid lemonade made maid masquerade paid parade persuade played promenade raid renegade serenade shade spade stockade suede tirade trade

graffiti agency artistry Audi bee bigotry certainty charity clemency CPT custody decree dignity DMZ Easy-E eulogy factory fee flea flee free gee glee GP he homey key knee me R&D plea pea sea see she tea thee theory tree trustee vulgarity we (see **be**)

grain (see **insane**)

gram (see **am**)

granny Annie canny fanny nanny

grape ape cape cityscape drape escape landscape rape seascape shape tape

grapevine align asinine assign benign combine concubine confine consign decline define design dine divine entwine feline fine incline line malign mine nine outshine pine porcupine recline refine resign Rhine shine shrine sign spine stein swine twine underline undermine vine whine wine

graph calf carafe epitaph giraffe paragraph phonograph photograph polygraph riffraff staff telegraph

grasp asp clasp gasp

grass alas amass ass bass brass class crass gas glass harass hourglass lass looking-glass mass morass mustache overpass pass sass surpass

gratitude attitude latitude platitude

grave behave brave cave concave crave engrave forgave gave knave pave rave save shave slave waive wave

gravel gavel ravel travel unravel

gravity cavity depravity

greed agreed breed centipede concede creed deed exceed feed heed inbreed knead lead mislead need precede proceed read recede reed secede seed speed stampede succeed Swede tweed weed

greedy beady needy seedy speedy weedy (see *be*)

green (see **mean**)

greet athlete beat beet bittersweet bleat cheat compete complete conceit concrete deceit defeat delete deplete discreet discrete eat elite feat

feet fleet heat incomplete indiscreet meat meet mistreat neat
obsolete parakeet receipt repeat retreat seat sheet sleet street suite
sweet treat wheat

grew (see **do**)

grief beef belief brief chief disbelief leaf relief thief

grieve achieve believe bereave conceive disbelieve eve heave leave
perceive receive relieve reprieve retrieve sleeve weave

grill bill chill daffodil distill drill fill frill fulfill gill hill ill imbecile instill kill mill
nil quill shrill sill skill spill still swill thrill till trill until whippoorwill will
windmill windowsill

grim brim dim Eminem gym him hymn limb pseudonym skim slim swim
trim whim

grin aspirin been begin Benjamin Berlin bin chagrin chin Crooklyn discipline
feminine fin 5x10 genuine gin heroine in inn kin mandolin
mannequin masculine moccasin origin pin saccharine shin sin skin
spin thick-and-thin thin tin twin violin win within

grip (see **trip**)

grocer closer (see *sir*)

groin coin Des Moines join loin purloin sirloin tenderloin

groove approve behoove disapprove disprove groove improve move
prove remove

gross adios bellicose close comatose diagnose dose engross grandiose
morose nose overdose varicose verbose

grouch couch crouch ouch pouch slouch vouch

ground (see **found**)

group coop droop dupe hoop loop nincompoop poop scoop sloop soup
stoop swoop troop troupe whoop

grovel hovel novel

grow (see **glow**)

grown (see **known**)

growth both loath oath overgrowth undergrowth

guard avant-garde bogard card chard discard disregard hard lard regard
retard tarred yard

guess access address baroness bashfulness bitterness bless caress chess
cleverness cloudiness compress confess craziness deadliness
depress digress distress dizziness dress duress eagerness easiness
eeriness emptiness excess express finesse foolish-ness happiness
haziness homelessness idleness impress joyfulness laziness less

limitless Loch Ness lustfulness mess nervousness obsess openness oppress outrageousness penniless playfulness possess press progress queasiness recess regress repossess repress rockiness seediness shallowness silkiness sleaziness sleepiness sneakiness SOS spaciousness spitefulness stress success suppress thoughtfulness transgress uselessness viciousness willingness worldliness yes youthfulness

guest (see **best**)

guilt built hilt jilt kilt quilt spilt stilt tilt Vanderbilt wilt

guitar A&R are bar bazaar bizarre car caviar cigar czar disbar far jar par radar scar sitar spar star tar

gull annul cull dull hull lull mull scull skull

gum (see **dumb**)

gumbo jumbo (see *no*)

gun anyone begun bun comparison done everyone fun Galveston hon Hun jettison none nun oblivion one outdone outrun over-done overrun phenomenon pun run shotgun shun simpleton skeleton son stun sun ton unison venison won

gust (see **trust**)

gut but butt coconut cut glut halibut hut King Tut mutt nut putt rut scuttlebutt shut slut smut strut uncut

gutter butter clutter cutter flutter mutter putter shutter sputter strutter stutter utter

guy alibi amplify banzai barfly butterfly buy by bye certify clarify crucify defy deify deny die dignify diversify dragonfly drive-by dry dye eye firefly fly fry FYI glorify gratify high horrify I identify imply July justify lie lullaby modify my mystify notify passerby pie pry qualify rely rye satisfy sci-fi shy sigh signify simplify sky sly specify spry spy terrify testify thigh tie try underlie verify why

gypsy dipsy Poughkeepsie tipsy

H

had ad add bad Brad cad Chad clad Dad egad fad glad grad lad mad nomad pad plaid sad shad Trinidad

hail (see **ale**)

hair (see **air**)

hairy carry hare Kari marry miscarry parry vary (see *cherry*)

hallow callow fallow mallow marshmallow shallow tallow

Halloween (see **mean**)

halt assault cobalt exalt fault malt salt somersault vault

hammer clamor damn 'er glamour grammar slammer sledgehammer stammer yammer

hand and band brand canned command contraband demand expand fanned grand land panned planned reprimand Rio Grande sand stand

handle candle dandle sandal scandal vandal

handy Andy brandy candy dandy randy sandy

hanky cranky hanky-panky lanky scanky Yankee

happiness (see **guess**)

happy crappie nappy pappy sappy scrappy slaphappy yappy

harbor arbor barber (see *door*)

hard avant-garde bogard card chard discard disregard guard lard regard retard tarred yard

hark aardvark arc ark bark dark embark lark mark narc park patriarch remark shark spark stark

Harlem call 'em haul 'em maul 'em stall 'em wall 'em

harm arm alarm charm disarm farm forearm

harmonic catatonic chronic diatonic enharmonic ironic monophonic philharmonic phonic platonic polyphonic sonic symphonic tonic

harp carp sharp

harsh marsh

has as jazz razzmatazz whereas

haste baste aftertaste braced chaste distaste faced freckle-faced hatchet-faced lambaste paste taste waist waste

hat (see **at**)

hatch attach batch catch detach dispatch latch match patch scratch snatch

hatchet latchet ratchet

hate (see **ate**)

hated anticipated bated belated dated fated grated mated rated related
     sedated skated x-rated (see **ate[d]**)

haunt daunt flaunt gaunt jaunt taunt want

haunting daunting flaunting jaunting taunting vaunting wanting

have calve

hawk (see **clock**)

haze ablaze amaze appraise bays blaze braze craze days daze faze gaze
     glaze graze malaise mayonnaise maze nays nowadays plays
     praise ways

hazy crazy daisy foogazy lazy scrazy

he (see **be**)

head ahead bed bedspread bread bred coed dead dread fed figurehead
     fled flowerbed fountainhead gingerbread inbred lead led misled
     misread overfed read red riverbed said shed shred sled sped spread
     thoroughbred thread underfed unthread wed

heal appeal automobile Bastille Camille conceal deal eel feel genteel he'll
     heel ideal kneel meal mobile peel real reel repeal reveal seal steel
     spiel squeal steal steel veal we'll wheal zeal

healer congealer dealer feeler reeler sealer squealer stealer wheeler
     (see *her*)

health commonwealth stealth wealth

hear (see **near**)

heard absurd bird blackbird bluebird curd herd hummingbird ladybird
     mockingbird overheard third word yellowbird

hearse adverse converse curse disburse disperse diverse immerse
     intersperse inverse nurse purse rehearse reverse terse transverse
     traverse universe verse worse

heart apart art cart chart counterpart dart depart mart part smart start
     sweetheart tart upstart

heartache (see **ache**)

heat (see **sweet**)

heaven eleven leaven 187 seven

heavy bevy Chevy levee

Heavy D (see **be**)

heck check Czech deck fleck neck peck Quebec speck trek wreck

height (see **flight**)

heist Christ diced iced zeitgeist
held felled meld upheld weld
hell bell belle Carmel carrousel cell clientele dell dwell excel farewell fell gel hotel infidel knell mademoiselle personnel sell shell smell spell tell well yell
hellbound hellhound spellbound (see *found*)
hellfire shellfire (see *fire*)
hellish embellish relish
hello bellow cello delo fellow Jell-O mellow Othello yellow
help kelp yelp
her amateur blur chauffeur concur confer connoisseur defer demur deter fur gansta incur infer Jennifer myrrh occur per prefer purr recur sir slur spur stir transfer voyageur were whir
Hercules (see **ease**)
here (see **near**)
hero Nero zero (see *know*)
hesitative (see **native**)
hey (see **say**)
hick arithmetic arsenic brick candlestick candlewick Catholic chick click copasetic flick heartsick kick lick limerick love-sick lunatic maverick medic nick pick sick slick stick thick tic tick wick
hid bid did forbid grid invalid lid Madrid pyramid rid skid slid squid
hide beside bona fide bride collide confide countryside decide defied died dignified divide eyed fireside guide hillside homicide inside lied outside override pride provide reside ride side slide snide stride subdivide subside suicide tide tried wide yuletide
higgler giggler wiggler (see *her*)
high (see **cry**)
highlight skylight twilight (see *light*)
highslidin' collidin' confidin' decidin' dividin' guidin' hidin' overridin' providin' residin' ridin' sidin' slidin' stridin' subdividin'
highway byway skyway (see *way*)
hijacker attacker backer blacker cracker hacker nutcracker packer ransacker slacker smacker tracker
hike bike like mike spike strike tyke
hilarious Aquarius gregarious precarious Sagittarius various (see *us*)
hill (see **fill**)

hilly Billy Chile Chili chilly dilly filly frilly hillbilly lily Philly Piccadilly piccalilli shrilly silly willy-nilly

him brim dim Eminem grim gym hymn limb pseudonym skim slim swim trim whim

hinge binge cringe fringe infringe singe

hint flint lint mint peppermint print spearmint splint sprint squint tint

hip (see **trip**)

hip-hop chop co-opt cop crop drop eavesdrop flop hop lollipop mop plop pop prop raindrop shop stop swap tip-top whop

hippie chippy dippy drippy flippy Mississippi nippy slippy snippy tippy yippee zippy

hire (see **fire**)

his biz fizz frizz is quiz showbiz 'tis whiz

hiss abyss amiss analysis armistice bliss carcass cowardice dis dismiss emphasis gangstress hypothesis kiss miss mistress nemesis office prejudice Swiss synthesis this

history mystery (see *be*)

hit befit bit fit 'git grit kit knit it jit legit lit nit-wit pit quit sit twit unfit wit zit

ho (see **know**)

hoagie Bogie stogie

hoard (see **lord**)

hoax chokes coax folks jokes smokes spokes yokes

hobby bobby knobby lobby snobby (see *be*)

hold behold blindfold bold centerfold cold fold foothold foretold gold household marigold mold old retold scold sold told uphold withhold

hole bowl buttonhole cajole casserole coal control dole droll enroll goal loophole Maypole mole Old King Cole oriole parole patrol pole poll porthole role roll scroll tadpole toll troll whole

holiday (see **say**)

hollow Apollo follow swallow wallow

Hollyhood (see **good**)

Hollywood (see **good**)

holy drolly lowly roly-poly solely wholly

home chrome chromosome comb dome foam gnome honeycomb metronome Nome poem roam Rome tome

homeboy annoy boy convoy corduroy coy decoy destroy employ enjoy joy Illinois ploy Roy Savoy soy toy troy

homegirl curl earl girl hurl pearl swirl twirl whirl

homey (see **be**)

honesty (see **be**)

honey bunny funny g-money money sunny

Honolulu Lulu Zulu

honor dishonor goner

hood (see **good**)

hook book brook cook crook look mistook nook outlook rook shook took undertook

hoop coop droop dupe group loop nincompoop poop scoop sloop soup stoop swoop troop troupe whoop

hope antelope cantaloupe cope dope elope envelope grope gyroscope horoscope kaleidoscope microscope mope pope rope scope slope soap stethoscope telescope

horn adorn airborne born Cape Horn Capricorn corn lovelorn Matterhorn morn mourn popcorn scorn stillborn sworn unicorn warn worn

horny corny thorny

horrify alibi amplify banzai barfly butterfly buy by bye certify clarify crucify defy deify deny die dignify diversify dragonfly drive-by dry dye eye firefly fly fry FTI glorify gratify guy high horrify I identify imply July justify lie lullaby modify my mystify notify passerby pie pry qualify rely rye satisfy sci-fi shy sigh signify simplify sky sly specify spry spy terrify testify thigh tie try underlie verify why

horror adorer explorer ignorer restorer roarer snorer soarer (see *her*)

horse coarse course divorce endorse force Norse reinforce remorse resource source

hoss across albatross boss cross double-cross floss gloss loss moss rhinoceros sauce toss

host boast coast foremost furthermost ghost innermost most post roast toast whipping post

hot apricot blot Camelot clot cot cybot dot forget-me-not forgot fought gavotte got hot-shot jot knot lot not plot pot robot rot shot slingshot somewhat spot squat swat tot trot watt what yacht

hotel bell belle Carmel carrousel cell clientele dell dwell excel farewell fell gel hell infidel knell mademoiselle personnel sell shell smell spell tell well yell

hound abound around astound background battleground bloodhound bound compound confound downed dumbfound found ground impound merry-go-round mound pound profound Oaktown renowned resound round sound spellbound surround under-.ground wound

hour devour flour our scour (see *flower*)

house blouse douse grouse louse madhouse mouse outhouse penthouse slaughterhouse souse spouse

how allow avow bough bow brow chow cow disavow endow frau kowtow now ow plough plow row slough somehow sow thou vow wow

howl cowl foul fowl growl jowl owl prowl scowl waterfowl

huff (see **bluff**)

hug bug drug dug jug lug mug plug pug rug shrug slug smug snug thug tug

huge centrifuge Scrooge stooge

hulk bulk sulk

hum (see **numb**)

human Harry S. Truman Paul Newman (see *man*)

humble bumble crumble fumble grumble humble jumble mumble rumble stumble tumble

humiliate affiliate conciliate

humor bloomer boomer consumer rumor tumor

hung (see **young**)

hunger fishmonger rumormonger younger (see *her*)

hunt affront blunt brunt bunt confront forefront front grunt punt runt shunt stunt

hurdle curdle girdle

hurricane (see **insane**)

hurry curry flurry fury jury Missouri scurry slurry surrey worry

hurt alert avert blurt concert convert curt curtain desert dessert dirt divert exert expert extrovert flirt insert introvert invert pervert shirt skirt squirt subvert yogurt

hustle bustle corpuscle muscle mussel rustle tussle

hydro (see **know**)

hype archetype gripe pipe prototype ripe stereotype stripe swipe type wipe

hysteric atmospheric cleric Derrick esoteric generic hemispheric hysteric numeric

H

i

I alibi amplify banzai barfly butterfly buy by bye certify clarify crucify cry defy deify deny die dignify diversify dragonfly drive-by dry dye eye firefly fly fry FYI glorify gratify guy high horrify identify imply July justify lie lullaby modify my mystify notify passerby pie pry qualify rely rye satisfy sci-fi shy sigh signify simplify sky sly specify spry spy terrify testify thigh tie try underlie verify why

ice advice concise device dice entice lice mice nice paradise precise price rice sacrifice spice splice suffice thrice twice vice

icicle bicycle tricycle

icy dicey spicy

idealist (see **exist**)

idiot (see **it**)

idol bridal bridle homicidal idle suicidal tidal

if cliff handkerchief sniff stiff tiff whiff

iffy jiffy sniffy spiffy

ignore (see **door**)

ignorant abandonment accident affluent ascendant attendant defendant dependent descendant reverent sacrament sediment sentiment settlement subsequent succulent incompetent independent pendant president prominent superintendent transcendent violent well-meant wonderment

ill bill chill daffodil distill drill fill frill fulfill gill grill hill imbecile instill kill mill nil quill shrill sill skill spill still swill thrill till trill until whippoorwill will windmill windowsill

illusion allusion conclusion confusion delusion fusion inclusion infusion seclusion transfusion

image scrimmage

imitative (see **native**)

immature (see **cure**)

imp blimp gimp limp pimp shrimp skimp wimp

impostor accoster foster lost 'er roster

impressive aggressive depressive digressive excessive expressive possessive progressive regressive successive

in aspirin been begin Benjamin Berlin bin chagrin chin Crooklyn discipline feminine fin 5x10 genuine gin grin heroine inn kin mandolin mannequin masculine moccasin origin pin saccharine shin sin skin spin thick-and-thin thin tin twin violin win within

inch cinch flinch lynch pinch

include brood clued conclude crude dude exclude food glued intrude misconstrued mood preclude prude rude seclude shrewd wooed

increase cease crease decease decrease fleece geese grease Greece lease masterpiece peace piece police release

independent ascendant attendant defendant dependent descendant independent pendant superintendent transcendent

individual residual

indulge bulge divulge

industry (see **be**)

infatuate (see **ate**)

inferior exterior interior superior ulterior

infernal colonel eternal external fraternal internal journal kernel maternal nocturnal paternal

inflict addict conflict constrict contradict convict derelict evict flicked licked predict pricked strict

influence (see **fence**)

influential confidential credential deferential differential essential existential nonessential potential preferential presidential providential prudential quintessential residential sequential torrential

inherit demerit disinherit (see *it*)

initial artificial beneficial judicial official sacrificial superficial

injure ginger infringer

injury (see **be**)

ink blink brink chink clink drink fink kink link mink pink rink shrink sink slink stink wink zinc

innuendo crescendo diminuendo Nintendo (see *know*)

insane abstain again airplane arraign ascertain attain brain Cain campaign cane chain champagne cocaine complain contain crane detain disdain domain drain entertain explain feign gain grain humane hurricane hydroplane lane main Maine maintain mane migraine obtain ordain pain pane pertain plain plane profane propane rain refrain reign rein remain sane slain Spain sprain stain strain sustain train vain vane vein wane windowpane

insecure (see **cure**)

I

insert (see **hurt**)

insist accompanist analyst anarchist anthropologist archeologist assist
biologist Calvinist capitalist coexist communist consist cyst desist
dismissed egoist essayist evangelist exist exorcist fatalist gist hissed
humanist humorist idealist imperialist journalist kissed list lobbyist
Methodist missed mist moralist motorist nationalist novelist organist
perfectionist pharmacist pianist plagiarist psychologist romanticist
satirist sentimentalist socialist soloist specialist strategist terrorist
theologist theorist twist ventriloquist vocalist wordsmith wrist

insisted (see **twisted**)

inspector collector connector deflector detector director injector nectar
objector projector prospector protector reflector selector vector
(see *her*)

inspiration congregational creational educational recreational sensational

inspire acquire admire amplifier aspire attire buyer choir conspire crier
cryer desire dire drier dryer entire esquire expire fire flier friar higher
hire inquire justifier liar magnifier multiplier mystifier perspire prior
prophesier require retire satisfier sire squire supplier testifier tire
transpire wire

insurance assurance endurance

intensive apprehensive comprehensive defensive expensive extensive
incomprehensive inexpensive offensive pensive

invasion abrasion dissuasion equation evasion occasion persuasion

invent (see **bent**)

invention (see **tension**)

inventive attentive inattentive incentive retentive

inventor center dissenter enter experimenter frequenter mentor presenter
preventer renter tormenter

invest arrest attest best breast chest congest crest detest digest divest
double-breast infest ingest interest jest manifest molest nest protest
quest request rest single-breast suggest test vest

invisible divisible indivisible visible

invite appetite bite blight bright byte contrite copyright daylight delight
despite dynamite excite Fahrenheit fight flight fright headlight
height ignite kite knight light midnight might moonlight night
outright parasite plight polite quite recite reunite right satellite sight
site sleight slight spite starlight sunlight tight trite twilight unite
white write

involve absolve devolve dissolve evolve revolve solve
irate gyrate (see *rate*)
iron Byron siren (see *in*)
ironic catatonic chronic diatonic enharmonic harmonic monophonic
    philharmonic phonic platonic polyphonic sonic symphonic tonic
is biz fizz frizz his quiz showbiz 'tis whiz
island highland (see *land*)
issue tissue (see *you*)
it befit bit fit 'git grit kit knit hit idiot jit legit lit nit-wit pit quit sit twit unfit
    wit zit
ivory (see **be**)

I

> Hip Hop is Hip Hop but it's not Hip Hop from
> before....It's not enough imagination. It's
> not an art anymore. I hear brothers
> freestyle and say the same thing like the
> next man talking about he's goin' to pull
> out his glock. Blazy blah what he goin' to
> do on the block. Anybody can do that. But
> he's just promoting violence. There's no
> skill there. The majority of it is gangster
> and I am getting tired of it. I never talked
> about killing in my rhymes. In fact no one
> did in those days.
>
> —Kota-Rock of the Fantastic Romantic Five

j

jack almanac attack back black Cadillac cardiac clickety-clack crack
egomaniac feedback hack Hackensack haystack jack kleptomaniac
knack lack mack maniac pack plaque Pontiac Prozac quack rack sack
shack slack snack stack tack track whack yak zodiac

jacket bracket packet racket (see **it**)

jail ale bail bale blackmail Braille cocktail curtail exhale fail female flail frail
hail hale impale inhale mail male nail pale prevail rail regale sail sale
scale shale snail stale tail they'll veil whale

jam (see **am**)

jank bank blank clank crank dank drank flank frank gank hank outrank plank
prank rank sank shank shrank skank spank stank tank thank yank

jar A&R are bar bazaar bizarre car caviar cigar czar disbar far guitar par radar
scar sitar spar star tar

jaw Arkansas awe bra caw claw draw flaw gnaw guffaw hurrah jaw law Ma
nah outlaw overdraw Pa paw raw saw seesaw shah slaw squaw
straw thaw withdraw

jazz as has razzmatazz whereas

jealous tell us zealous (see **us**)

jealousy (see **be**)

jelly belly celly deli Kelly Nelly Shelly smelly

jerk clerk handiwork irk Kirk lurk murk overwork perk quirk shirk smirk Turk work

jester Chester contester fester investor Lester molester pester protester
semester sequester tester Westchester Winchester

jet (see **met**)

jewel cruel duel fuel

jiggle giggle squiggle wiggle wriggle

jiggy Biggie ciggy piggy twiggy

jing anything bling-bling bring cling ding evening everything fling jing king
ring sing sling spring sting string swing thing wing wring

jingle intermingle Kris Kringle mingle shingle single tingle

jinx lynx minks sphinx thinks winks

jit befit bit fit 'git grit kit knit hit it legit lit mitt nit-wit pit quit sit twit unfit
ultimate wit zit

job blob bob cob fob gob hob hobnob job knob lob mob nob rob slob
snob sob swab throb

jock Bangkok beanstalk boondock clock cock cornstalk crock deadlock dreadlock defrock dock flintlock flock frock gawk glock gridlock hawk hock J. S. Bach knock Little Rock livestock lock mock Mohawk padlock peacock rock shock sidewalk small talk Tupoc smock sock squawk stalk stock talk tomahawk unlock walk wok

Joe (see **glow**)

join adjoin coin Des Moines groin loin purloin sirloin tenderloin

joint anoint appoint counterpoint disappoint disjoint

joke artichoke baroque bloke broke choke cloak coke croak evoke folk invoke oak poke provoke revoke smoke soak spoke stroke toke woke yoke

joker broker choker mediocre poker provoker revoker smoker stoker stroker woke 'er

jolly collie dolly finale folly golly melancholy Molly Polly tamale trolley volley

jolt bolt colt dolt revolt thunderbolt

journal colonel eternal external fraternal infernal internal kernel maternal nocturnal paternal

journalist (see **exist**)

journey attorney tourney (see *be*)

joy annoy boy convoy corduroy coy decoy destroy employ enjoy homeboy Illinois ploy Roy Savoy soy toy troy

judge budge drudge fudge grudge misjudge nudge smudge

juggle smuggle snuggle struggle

juice abuse accuse confuse cues deduce diffuse disuse duce excuse induce infuse introduce juice misuse obtuse peruse produce profuse reduce refuse reproduce seduce Syracuse use

jumbo gumbo (see *no*)

jump bump chump clump dump hump lump plump rump slump stump thump trump ump

junction conjunction function injunction

june attune commune dune immune impugn inopportune tune (see *moon*)

jungle bungle

junk bunk chunk clunk crunk cyberpunk drunk dunk flunk funk g-funk hunk monk p-funk plunk punk shrunk skunk slunk spunk stunk sunk trunk

juror deferrer demurrer furor incurrer stirrer (see *her*)

jury curry flurry fury hurry Missouri scurry slurry surrey worry

just adjust August bust crust dust disgust distrust encrust entrust gust lust mistrust must robust rust thrust trust unjust

juvenile (see **smile**)

k

kamikaze (see **be**)

karena arena Athena concertina hyena subpoena Tina

keep barkeep cheep creep deep heap leap peep reap seep sheep sleep steep sweep weep

keg beg egg leg peg

kept accept adept crept except intercept overslept slept stepped swept wept

key (see **be**)

kick arithmetic arsenic brick candlestick candlewick Catholic chick click copasetic flick heartsick hick lick limerick love-sick lunatic maverick medic nick pick sick slick stick thick tic tick wick

kid bid did forbid grid hid invalid lid Madrid pyramid rid skid slid squid

kill (see **fill**)

killer caterpillar chiller distiller driller filler instiller pillar shriller spiller swiller thriller tiller

killing (see **willing**)

kin aspirin been begin Benjamin Berlin bin chagrin chin Crooklyn discipline feminine fin 5x10 genuine gin grin heroine in inn mandolin mannequin masculine moccasin origin pin saccharine shin sin skin spin thick-and-thin thin tin twin violin win within

kind behind bind blind find grind hind humankind mastermind mind remind signed unkind unwind wind wined

kindle dwindle rekindle spindle swindle

king anything bling-bling bring cling ding evening everything fling jing ring sing sling spring sting string swing thing wing wring (add "-ing" to action words, e.g., run[ning], etc.)

kingdom (see **dumb**)

kinky blinky dinky pinky slinky stinky

kiss abyss amiss analysis armistice carcass cowardice dis dismiss emphasis hiss gangstress hypothesis miss mistress nemesis office prejudice Swiss synthesis this

kissing dismissing dissing hissing missing reminiscing

kit befit bit fit 'git grit knit hit idiot jit it legit lit nit-wit pit quit sit twit unfit wit zit

kite appetite bite blight bright byte contrite copyright daylight delight despite dynamite excite Fahrenheit fight flight fright headlight height ignite invite kite knight light midnight might moonlight night outright parasite plight polite quite recite reunite right satellite sight site sleight slight spite starlight sunlight tight trite twilight unite white write

kitten bitten Briton mitten smitten written (see *in*)

kitty city committee ditty gritty pity pretty self-pity witty

knee (see **be**)

knew adieu anew avenue barbecue bayou chew cue curfew debut dew due ensue ewe few guru honeydew hue I.O.U. imbue ingénue interview Jew lieu new Nehru overdue pee-ewe pew preview pursue renew residue revenue review spew subdue sue undue view yew you (see *do*)

knight (see **light**)

knife afterlife jackknife life strife wife

knob blob bob cob fob gob hob hobnob job lob mob nob rob slob snob sob swab throb

knock (see **clock**)

knot apricot blot Camelot clot cot cybot dot forget-me-not forgot fought gavotte got hot hot-shot jot lot not plot pot robot rot shot slingshot somewhat spot squat swat tot trot watt what yacht

know afro although banjo beau below bestow blow bow buffalo bungalow calico crossbow crow depot doe domino dough embryo escrow Eskimo flow foe forgo fro gazebo gigolo glow go grow heigh ho ho-ho hobo hoe hydro incognito indigo Joe long-ago low Mexico mistletoe mow no oboe oh outgrow overflow overgrow overthrow owe Pinocchio plateau quo rainbow ratio roe row sew slow snow so Soho status quo stow studio though throw tiptoe to-and-fro toe Tokyo tow tremolo undergo undertow vertigo woe yo yo-yo

knowledge acknowledge college (see *ledge*)

known alone atone backbone baritone blown bone chaperone clone condone cone cornerstone cyclone flown full-blown full-grown gramophone grindstone groan grown headstone k-tone loan lone microphone milestone moan monotone mown overgrown overthrown own phone postpone prone saxophone sewn shown stone telephone thrown tone trombone unknown xylophone zone

k

knuckle arbuckle buckle chuckle honeysuckle suckle
Koran an ban can can-can Dan fan Iran man Nan plan Tehran
kosher so sure (see *her*)
k-tone alone atone backbone baritone blown bone chaperone clone
condone cone cornerstone cyclone flown full-blown full-grown
gramophone grindstone groan grown headstone known loan lone
microphone milestone moan monotone mown overgrown
overthrown own phone postpone prone saxophone sewn shown
stone telephone thrown tone trombone unknown xylophone zone

I'm actually responsible for playing the
drums on the turntable. Not just letting
drums play, but playing the kick and the
snare in real time. As a band, Qbert,
Apollo, and I were responsible for
actually making the turntable into
different instruments. Picking up
guitar strums and actually playing them
as a guitar. Picking up flute and
horns. Playing the saxophone and
scratching a sax so it actually
sounds like a saxophone.
—MixMaster Mike of the Beastie Boys

Turntable Technique: The Art of the DJ
by Stephen Webber

l

lab blab cab crab dab drab fab gab grab jab nab scab slab stab tab
label (see **able**)
labor belabor neighbor saber
lace ace base bass brace case chase commonplace debase disgrace
　　　 displace embrace encase erase face grace mace misplace pace
　　　 place race replace space steeplechase trace unlace vase
lack almanac attack back black Cadillac cardiac clickety-clack crack
　　　 egomaniac feedback hack Hackensack haystack jack
　　　 kleptomaniac knack mack maniac pack plaque Pontiac
　　　 Prozac quack rack sack shack slack snack stack tack track
　　　 whack yak zodiac
lad (see **mad**)
lame acclaim aim became blame came claim exclaim fame flame frame
　　　 game inflame maim name proclaim same shame tame
lamp amp camp champ clamp cramp damp ramp stamp vamp
land and band brand canned command contraband demand expand
　　　 fanned grand hand panned planned reprimand Rio Grande
　　　 sand stand
lane (see **rain**)
large barge charge discharge enlarge
lark aardvark arc ark bark dark embark hark mark narc park patriarch
　　　 remark shark spark stark
laser appraiser blazer gazer maser phaser praiser razor stargazer
lash ash balderdash bash brash cash clash crash dash flash gash gnash
　　　 rash rehash slash smash splash stash thrash trash
last aghast blast cast classed contrast fast flabbergast forecast gassed mast
　　　 outlast overcast passed past vast
late (see **ate**)
latin battin' cattin' fatten flatten Manhattan paten Patton
latitude attitude gratitude platitude
laugh calf carafe epitaph giraffe graph paragraph phonograph photograph
　　　 polygraph riffraff staff telegraph
laughter after grafter hereafter rafter thereafter
lawn (see **dawn**)
lazy crazy daisy foogazy hazy scrazy

L

lead ahead bed bedspread bread bred coed dead dread fed figurehead
fled flowerbed fountainhead gingerbread head inbred led misled
misread overfed read red riverbed said shed shred sled sped spread
thoroughbred thread underfed unthread wed

leaf beef belief brief chief disbelief grief relief thief

league fatigue intrigue

leak beak bleak creek eek freak geek meek reek seek speak tweak weak
week

lean (see **mean**)

leap barkeep cheep creep deep heap keep peep reap seep sheep sleep
steep sweep weep

learn adjourn burn churn concern discern earn fern intern kern overturn
return sojourn spurn stern taciturn turn urn yearn

leash quiche unleash

least beast ceased creased deceased east feast pieced priest yeast

leather altogether feather Heather tether together weather whether
(see *her*)

leave achieve believe bereave conceive disbelieve eve grieve heave
perceive receive relieve reprieve retrieve sleeve weave

lecture architecture conjecture

ledge allege dredge edge fledge hedge privilege sacrilege sledge wedge

left deft theft

legal beagle eagle illegal regal sea gull

legit befit bit fit 'git grit kit knit hit it jit legit lit mitt nit-wit pit quit sit twit unfit
ultimate wit zit

leisure seizure

lend (see **friend**)

length strength

less access address baroness bashfulness bitterness bless caress chess
cleverness cloudiness compress confess craziness deadliness
depress digress distress dizziness dress duress eagerness easiness
eeriness emptiness excess express finesse foolishness guess
happiness haziness homelessness idleness impress joyfulness
laziness limitless Loch Ness lustfulness mess nervousness obsess
openness oppress outrageousness penniless playfulness possess
press progress queasiness recess regress repossess repress
rockiness seediness shallowness silkiness sleaziness sleepiness
sneakiness SOS spaciousness spitefulness stress success suppress

thoughtfulness transgress uselessness viciousness willingness worldliness yes youthfulness

let (see **met**)

letter better cheddar debtor getter setter sweater wetter

level bedevil bevel devil dishevel level revel

lewd (see **feud**)

Lex BMX complex decks duplex DMX ex flex hex necks pecks reflex Rolodex sex specs Tex unisex

liar amplifier beautifier briar buyer crier cryer drier dryer flier friar higher mystifier occupier prior simplifier slyer supplier testifier (see *fire*)

liberty (see **be**)

librarian (see **vegetarian**)

lick arithmetic arsenic brick candlestick candlewick Catholic chick click copasetic flick heartsick hick kick limerick love-sick lunatic maverick medic nick pick sick slick stick thick tic tick wick

lid bid did forbid grid hid invalid kid Madrid pyramid rid skid slid squid

lie alibi amplify banzai barfly butterfly buy by bye certify clarify crucify cry defy deify deny die dignify diversify dragonfly drive-by dry dye eye firefly fly fry FYI glorify gratify guy high horrify I identify imply July justify lullaby modify my mystify notify passerby pie pry qualify rely rye satisfy sci-fi shy sigh signify simplify sky sly specify spry spy terrify testify thigh tie try underlie verify why

lied (see **bride**)

lies advertise advise analyze apologize arise authorize baptize capitalize capsize characterize comprise compromise criticize demise deputize despise devise dies disguise economize emphasize enterprise epitomize eulogize excise exercise exorcise eyes familiarize fertilize flies generalize hypnotize idealize idolize immortalize improvise italicize legalize materialize memorize merchandise minimize neutralize ostracize paralyze patronize penalize personalize philosophize plagiarize prize rationalize realize recognize reprise revise rise satirize scandalize scrutinize size socialize specialize spies sterilize stigmatize subsidize summarize sunrise supervise surmise surprise sympathize terrorize theorize thighs ties tranquilize utilize verbalize visualize vocalize wise

life afterlife jackknife knife strive wife

lift drift gift shift spendthrift swift thrift

light appetite bite blight bright byte contrite copyright daylight delight
          despite dynamite excite Fahrenheit fight flight fright headlight height
          ignite invite kite knight midnight might moonlight night outright
          parasite plight polite quite recite reunite right satellite sight site
          sleight slight spite starlight sunlight tight trite twilight unite white write
like bike hike mike spike strike tyke
liking biking disliking spiking striking Viking
lily Billy Chile Chili chilly dilly filly frilly hillbilly hilly Philly Piccadilly piccalilli
          shrilly silly willy-nilly
limb brim dim Eminem grim gym hymn pseudonym skim slim swim trim whim
limber timber timbre
lime climb crime dime I'm pantomime prime rhyme slime summertime
          thyme time
limp blimp gimp pimp shrimp skimp wimp
line (see **fine**)
lingo bingo dingo flamingo gringo jingo (see *glow*)
lion buyin' cryin' dandelion denyin' dyin' lyin' Orion Ryan sighin' tryin' Zion
          (see *in*)
list (see **mist**)
listen christen dissin' glisten hissin' kissin' missin'
lit befit bit fit 'git grit kit knit hit it jit legit mitt nit-wit pit quit sit twit unfit
          ultimate wit zit
live affirmative alternative argumentative combative competitive consecutive
          conservative definitive expletive figurative forgive fugitive give
          informative intuitive lucrative narrative negative positive primitive
          prohibitive provocative relative representative sensitive talkative
          tentative
livid vivid
lizard blizzard gizzard scissored wizard
load (see **road**)
loan (see **lone**)
local focal vocal yokel
lock Bangkok beanstalk boondock clock cock cornstalk crock deadlock
          defrock dock dreadlock flintlock flock frock gawk glock gridlock hawk
          hock J. S. Bach jock knock Little Rock livestock mock Mohawk
          padlock peacock rock shock sidewalk small talk Tupoc smock sock
          squawk stalk stock talk tomahawk unlock walk wok

lock-down brown clown crown down downtown drown frown gown hand-me-down noun Oaktown renown town tumble-down upside down uptown

locket docket hocket pocket rocket socket sprocket (see *it*)

lodge dislodge dodge hodgepodge lodge

loft aloft oft soft

London undone (see *done*)

lone alone atone backbone baritone blown bone chaperone clone condone cone cornerstone cyclone flown full-blown full-grown gramophone grindstone groan grown headstone known k-tone loan microphone milestone moan monotone mown overgrown overthrown own phone postpone prone saxophone sewn shown stone telephone thrown tone trombone unknown xylophone zone

loner condoner donor groaner honer known 'er loan 'er loaner moaner owner phone 'er toner

long along belong bong ding-dong gong Hong Kong ping-pong prong song strong throng wrong

longing belonging prolonging wronging

look book brook cook crook hook mistook nook outlook rook shook took undertook

looking booking cooking hooking rooking

loon (see *moon*)

loose ace-deuce caboose goose juice moose noose papoose recluse spruce truce vamoose

lord aboard accord afford award board bored ford harpsichord hoard overboard poured reward shuffleboard soared sword ward

Los Angeles exodus helluva mess man jealous romances us scandalous unanimous unscramble us

lose blues booze bruise choose cruise news ooze snooze whose

loss across albatross boss cross double-cross floss hoss gloss moss rhinoceros sauce toss

lost bossed cost crossed exhaust flossed frost holocaust Pentecost tossed

lot (see **hot**)

lottery pottery watery

loud allowed aloud cloud crowd enshroud plowed proud shroud thundercloud

louder chowder powder prouder (see *her*)

L

lounge scrounge
love above dove glove ladylove mourning dove of shove turtle dove
lover cover discover hover recover rediscover shover undercover (see *her*)
low (see **blow**)
loyal broil coil foil oil recoil royal spoil toil turmoil
loyalty royalty (see *be*)
luck amuck buck chuck cluck deduct duck horror-struck muck pluck potluck
       puck struck suck truck tuck
lucky ducky Kentucky unlucky
lumber cucumber cumber encumber number slumber umber
lump bump chump clump dump hump jump plump rump slump stump
       thump trump ump
lunar communer crooner harpooner lampooner pruner schooner sooner
       spooner tuner
lunch brunch bunch crunch hunch munch punch scrunch
lure (see **cure**)
lust adjust August bust crust dust disgust distrust encrust entrust gust just
       mistrust must robust rust thrust trust unjust
luxury (see *be*)
lynch cinch flinch inch pinch
lyrical empirical miracle satirical

> If I offend anyone or whatever, I'm
> saying it so I'm willing to deal with
> it. I don't know if anybody does it like
> me, saying whatever they want to say. If
> I'm feeling it, then I'm gonna say it.
> Music is a form of expression.
>
> —Eminem

m

machine (see **mean**)

machinery beanery greenery scenery

mack almanac attack back black Cadillac cardiac clickety-clack crack
egomaniac feedback hack Hackensack haystack jack kleptomaniac
knack lack mack maniac pack plaque Pontiac Prozac quack rack sack
shack slack snack stack tack track whack yak zodiac

mad ad add bad Brad cad Chad clad Dad egad fad glad grad had lad
nomad pad plaid sad shad Trinidad

made afraid aid arcade barricade blade blockade braid brayed brigade
charade crusade degrade dismayed dissuade downgrade escapade
evade fade grade grenade hayed invade laid lemonade maid
masquerade paid parade persuade played promenade raid renegade
serenade shade spade stockade suede tirade trade

Madonna belladonna Donna iguana prima donna wanna

magic tragic (see *tick*)

magician (see *tradition*)

mail (see **ale**)

main abstain again airplane arraign ascertain attain brain Cain campaign
cane chain champagne cocaine complain contain crane detain
disdain domain drain entertain explain feign gain grain humane
hurricane hydroplane insane lane Maine maintain mane migraine
obtain ordain pain pane pertain plain plane profane propane rain
refrain reign rein remain sane slain Spain sprain stain strain sustain
train vain vane vein wane windowpane

major cager pager stager wager

make ache bake brake break cake fake flake forsake headache heartache wake
keepsake mistake opaque quake rake sake shake snake stake steak take

male (see **ale**)

malice Alice chalice Dallas palace phallus

mall all ball bawl brawl call crawl doll drawl fall gall haul install maul
Montreal nightfall overhaul parasol pitfall protocol rainfall scrawl
shawl small snowfall sprawl stall tall thrall wall waterfall y'all

malt assault cobalt exalt fault halt salt somersault vault

mamma Bahama comma Dalai Lama drama llama melodrama
pajama Yokohama

man ban can can-can Dan fan Iran Nan plan ran Tehran

maneuver Hoover mover prover remover Vancouver

manic (see **volcanic**)

manor banner canner fanner manner planner scanner spanner tanner

manual annual

many any Benny Jenny penny

map cap chap clap dap flap gap handicap lap mishap nap rap sap scrap slap snap strap tap trap wrap zap

maple papal staple

marble bull cock-and-bull do-able full pull wool (see *beautiful*)

march arch parch starch

mark aardvark arc ark bark dark embark hark lark narc park patriarch remark shark spark stark

marquee malarkey marquis oligarchy patriarchy

marriage carriage disparage miscarriage

marry carry hairy hare Kari miscarry parry vary (see *cherry*)

martyr barter Carter charter darter garter smarter starter tarter

mash ash balderdash bash brash cash clash crash dash flash gash gnash lash rash rehash slash smash splash stash thrash trash

mask ask bask cask flask task

match attach batch catch detach dispatch hatch latch patch scratch snatch

mate (see **ate**)

material cereal immaterial managerial ministerial serial

math aftermath bath homeopath path psychopath sociopath wrath

matrimony acrimony alimony baloney bony crony macaroni patrimony phony pony sanctimony stony testimony Tony

matrix (see **mix**)

may (see **say**)

mayor betrayer conveyor grayer layer payer player portrayer prayer slayer soothsayer sprayer stayer surveyor

me (see **be**)

mean bean between caffeine canteen chlorine clean codeine Colleen convene cuisine dean demean evergreen Florentine foreseen gasoline Gene green guillotine Halloween in-between intervene kerosene lean lien machine marine mezzanine Nazarene nectarine nicotine obscene preen quarantine queen ravine routine sardine scene seen serene spleen submarine tambourine tangerine teen thirteen (etc.) Vaseline velveteen wintergreen wolverine

meant (see **bent**)

measure displeasure pleasure treasure

meat (see **meet**)

mecca Rebecca Tribeca (see *raw, zebra*)

mechanical botanical manacle tyrannical

medium tedium (see *some*)

meek beak bleak creek eek freak geek leak reek seek speak tweak weak week

meet athlete beat beet bittersweet bleat cheat compete complete conceit concrete deceit defeat delete deplete discreet discrete eat elite feat feet fleet greet heat incomplete indiscreet meat meet mistreat neat obsolete parakeet receipt repeat retreat seat sheet sleet street suite sweet treat wheat

melancholy collie dolly finale folly golly jolly Molly Polly tamale trolley volley

mellow bellow cello delo fellow hello Jell-O Othello yellow

melodic episodic methodic periodic

melody (see **be**)

melon gellin' felon sellin' tellin' rebellin' yellin' (see *villain*)

melt belt Celt dealt felt heartfelt pelt welt

member December dismember ember November remember September

memory (see **be**)

men amen citizen den fen hen hydrogen Ken oxygen pen regimen specimen ten then yen Zen

menace tennis

mend (see **friend**)

menial congenial

mental accidental coincidental complemental continental dental departmental detrimental experimental fundamental gentle governmental incidental intercontinental lentil monumental Oriental parental regimental rental rudimental sentimental supplemental temperamental

mess access address baroness bashfulness bitterness bless caress chess cleverness cloudiness compress confess craziness deadliness depress digress distress dizziness dress duress eagerness easiness eeriness emptiness excess express finesse foolishness guess happiness haziness homelessness idleness impress joyfulness laziness less limitless Loch Ness lustfulness nervousness obsess openness oppress outrageousness penniless playfulness possess press progress queasiness recess regress repossess repress rockiness seediness shallowness silkiness sleaziness sleepiness sneakiness SOS spaciousness spitefulness stress success suppress thoughtfulness transgress uselessness viciousness willingness worldliness yes youthfulness

messiah Jeremiah Maya papaya

met alphabet bayonet bet brunette cabinet cadet cigarette clarinet cornet corvette debt duet epithet etiquette forget fret gazette get jet Joliet Juliet let luncheonette marionette net omelet pet quartet regret roulette set silhouette Somerset sunset sweat threat Tibet toilette upset vet 'vette violet wet yet

metal kettle mettle petal resettle settle

mice advice concise device dice entice ice lice nice paradise precise price rice sacrifice spice splice suffice thrice twice vice

middle diddle fiddle griddle riddle twiddle

midget digit fidget widget

might (see **night**)

M

mild child dialed piled smiled wild

mile (see **smile**)

military (see **ordinary**)

milk bilk ilk silk

million billion Brazilian Maximillian pavilion reptilian trillion zillion

millionaire (see **air**)

mind behind bind blind find grind hind humankind kind mastermind remind signed unkind unwind wind wined

mine align asinine assign benign combine concubine confine consign decline define design dine divine entwine feline fine grapevine incline line malign nine outshine pine porcupine recline refine resign Rhine shine shrine sign spine stein swine twine underline undermine vine whine wine

mingle intermingle jingle Kris Kringle shingle single tingle

miniature (see **pure**)

minister administer sinister

minor cosigner Carolina designer diner eyeliner finer liner miner nina refiner shiner signer

mint flint hint lint spearmint peppermint print splint sprint squint tint

minus sinus (see *us*)

minute spinet (see *it*)

miracle empirical lyrical satirical

mirage barrage camouflage garage entourage

mirror cheerer clearer dearer hearer jeerer nearer queerer severer sneerer spearer

misery (see **be**)

miss abyss amiss analysis armistice bliss carcass cowardice dis dismiss
emphasis gangstress hiss hypothesis kiss mistress nemesis office
prejudice Swiss synthesis this

missile bristle dismissal gristle missal sisal thistle whistle

mission (see **tradition**)

mist accompanist analyst anarchist anthropologist archeologist assist
biologist Calvinist capitalist coexist communist consist cyst desist
dismissed egoist essayist evangelist exist exorcist fatalist gist hissed
humanist humorist idealist imperialist insist journalist kissed list
lobbyist Methodist missed moralist motorist nationalist novelist
organist perfectionist pharmacist pianist plagiarist psychologist
romanticist satirist sentimentalist socialist soloist specialist strategist
terrorist theologist theorist twist ventriloquist vocalist wordsmith wrist

mistake ache bake brake break cake fake flake forsake headache
heartache keepsake make opaque quake rake shake snake stake
steak take wake

mistaken achin' bacon forsaken Jamaican makin' overtaken shaken
undertaken taken unshaken waken

mister assister blister resister sister twister (see *her*)

misty Christie Corpus Christi twisty (see *tea*)

mitt befit bit fit 'git grit kit knit hit it jit legit lit nit-wit pit quit sit twit unfit
ultimate wit zit

mix acrobatics bics crucifix fiddlesticks fix kicks licks matrix mathematics nix
picks politics six sticks Styx ticks transfix tricks wicks

mixer elixir fixer (see *her*)

mixture fixture

moan alone atone backbone baritone blown bone chaperone clone
condone cone cornerstone cyclone flown full-blown full-grown
gramophone grindstone groan grown headstone known k-tone loan
lone microphone milestone monotone mown overgrown overthrown
own phone postpone prone saxophone sewn shown stone
telephone thrown tone trombone unknown xylophone zone

M

mob blob bob cob fob gob hob hobnob job knob lob nob rob slob snob
    sob swab throb

mobster lobster

mock (see **shock**)

model coddle remodel swaddle toddle twaddle waddle

mogul ogle

moist hoist joist rejoiced voiced

mojo afro although banjo beau below bestow blow bow buffalo bungalow
    calico crossbow crow depot doe domino dough embryo escrow
    Eskimo flow foe forgo fro gazebo gigolo glow go grow heigh-ho ho-
    ho hobo hoe incognito indigo Joe know long ago low Mexico
    mistletoe mow no oboe oh outgrow overflow overgrow overthrow
    owe Pinocchio plateau quo rainbow ratio roe row sew slow snow so
    Soho status quo stow studio though throw tiptoe to-and-fro toe
    Tokyo tow tremolo undergo undertow vertigo woe yo yo-yo

molester Chester contester fester investor jester Lester pester protester
    semester sequester tester Westchester Winchester

mom aplomb bomb calm embalm Guam palm psalm qualm

Monday one day Sunday (see *day*)

money bunny funny g-money honey runny sunny

monk bunk chunk clunk crunk cyberpunk drunk dunk flunk funk hunk junk
    p-funk plunk punk shrunk skunk slunk spunk stunk sunk trunk

monkey chunky flunky funky spunky

mood brood clued conclude crude dude exclude food glued include intrude
    misconstrued mood preclude prude rude seclude shrewd wooed

moon afternoon baboon balloon bassoon boon buffoon cartoon cocoon
    coon croon goon harpoon harvest moon honeymoon lagoon
    lampoon loon maroon monsoon noon platoon prune raccoon
    saloon soon spittoon swoon tycoon typhoon (see *tune*)

moose ace-deuce caboose goose juice loose noose papoose recluse
    spruce truce vamoose

mop (see **drop**)

moral aural choral floral immoral laurel oral

more (see **door**)

mortal chortle immortal portal

most boast coast foremost furthermost ghost host innermost post roast
    toast whipping post

mother another brother other smother

motion commotion emotion locomotion lotion notion ocean potion promotion

motive emotive locomotive

motto blotto grotto legato staccato

mound (see **found**)

mountain countin' fountain

mourn adorn airborne born Cape Horn Capricorn forlorn forsworn horn lovelorn Matterhorn morn popcorn scorn sea borne stillborn sworn unicorn warn worn

mouse blouse douse grouse house louse madhouse outhouse penthouse slaughterhouse souse spouse

move approve behoove disapprove disprove groove improve prove remove

movie groovy

mow (see **blow**)

much clutch crutch Dutch hutch inasmuch retouch such touch

muck (see **truck**)

mud blood bud cud dud flood mud scud spud stud thud

muffin buffin' puffin ragamuffin stuffin' toughen

muffle duffle ruffle scuffle shuffle truffle

mug bug drug dug jug hug lug plug pug rug shrug snug slug snug thug tug

mule molecule ridicule vestibule Yule

mumble bumble crumble fumble grumble humble jumble mumble rumble stumble tumble

mural extramural intramural neural plural rural

murder girder herder

muscle bustle corpuscle hustle mussel rustle tussle

music arsenic brick candlestick Catholic chick click copastetic flick heartsick hick kick lick limerick love-sick maverick medic nick pick sick slick stick thick tic tick

musician (see **tradition**)

muss (see **us**)

must adjust August bust crust dust disgust distrust encrust entrust gust just lust mistrust robust rust thrust trust unjust

my (see **cry**)

mystery history

n

nail (see **ale**)

name acclaim aim became blame came claim exclaim fame flame frame game inflame lame maim proclaim same shame tame

nann an ban can can-can Dan fan Iran man plan ran Tehran

narc aardvark arc ark bark dark embark hark lark mark park patriarch remark shark spark stark

narcotic chaotic erotic exotic hypnotic idiotic macrobiotic quixotic

narrate (see **ate**)

narrow arrow barrow harrow marrow sparrow tarot

national international irrational rational passional

native accumulative appreciative authoritative communicative creative decorative generative hesitative imitative innovative investigative operative vindictive

natty addy caddie daddy fatty maddy patty

naughty dotty knotty manicotti spotty

near adhere appear atmosphere auctioneer beer bombardier career cashier cavalier chandelier cheer clear dear deer disappear ear engineer fear financier frontier gear hear hemisphere here insincere interfere jeer lavaliere leer mere mountaineer overhear overseer peer persevere pioneer queer racketeer reappear rear revere seer severe shear sheer sincere smear sneer spear sphere stratosphere tear veneer volunteer year

neat (see **meet**)

necessary (see **ordinary**)

neck check Czech deck fleck heck peck Quebec speck trek wreck

need agreed breed centipede concede creed deed exceed feed greed heed inbreed knead lead mislead precede proceed read recede reed secede seed speed stampede succeed Swede tweed weed

neglect (see **effect**)

neighbor belabor labor saber

neither breather either

Nelly celly deli jelly Kelly Shelly smelly

neon eon peon (see *dawn*)

nerve conserve curve deserve observe preserve reserve serve swerve

nest (see *best*)

never clever endeavor ever forever however lever sever whatever whenever wherever whoever

new adieu anew avenue barbecue bayou chew cue curfew debut dew due ensue ewe few guru honeydew hue I.O.U. imbue ingénue interview Jew knew new Nehru overdue pee-ewe pew preview pursue renew residue revenue review spew subdue sue undue view yew you (see *do*)

New York cork fork pitchfork pork stork torque uncork

next context flexed pretext text vexed

nibble dribble kibble quibble scribble Sibyl

nice advice concise device dice entice ice lice paradise precise price rice sacrifice spice splice suffice thrice twice vice

night appetite bite blight bright byte contrite copyright daylight delight despite dynamite excite Fahrenheit fight flight fright headlight height ignite invite kite knight light midnight might moonlight outright parasite plight polite quite recite reunite right satellite sight site sleight slight spite starlight sunlight tight trite twilight unite white write

nightmare (see **air**)

Nile (see **smile**)

nina cosigner Carolina designer diner eyeliner finer liner miner minor nina refiner shiner signer

nine align asinine assign benign combine concubine confine consign decline define design dine divine entwine fine incline line malign mine nine outshine pine porcupine recline refine resign Rhine shine shrine sign spine stein swine twine underline undermine vine whine wine

Nirvana Americana banana bandanna Diana Hannah Havana hosanna Indiana Louisiana Pollyanna Savannah Texarkana

no afro although banjo beau below bestow blow bow buffalo bungalow calico crossbow crow depot doe domino dough embryo escrow Eskimo flow foe forgo fro gazebo gigolo glow go grow heigh-ho ho-ho hobo hoe incognito indigo Joe know long ago low Mexico mistletoe mojo mow oboe oh outgrow overflow overgrow overthrow owe Pinocchio plateau quo rainbow ratio roe row sew slow snow so Soho status quo stow studio though throw tiptoe to-and-fro toe Tokyo tow tremolo undergo undertow vertigo woe yo yo-yo

nobody body embody gaudy lawdy shoddy somebody toddy

nocturnal colonel eternal external fraternal infernal internal journal kernel
        maternal paternal
nod abroad applaud awed broad clod cod defraud façade fraud god
        guffawed Izod odd pod prod promenade quad rod roughshod shod
        sod squad trod wad
noise boys poise Royce toys
none anyone begun bun comparison done everyone fun Galveston gun
        hon Hun jettison nun oblivion one outdone outrun over-done
        overrun phenomenon pun run shotgun shun simpleton skeleton son
        stun sun ton unison venison won
noodle boodle caboodle doodle feudal poodle Yankee Doodle
noon afternoon baboon balloon bassoon boon buffoon cartoon cocoon
        coon croon goon harpoon harvest moon honeymoon lagoon
        lampoon loon maroon monsoon moon platoon prune raccoon
        saloon soon spittoon swoon tycoon typhoon (see *tune*)
noose ace-deuce caboose goose juice loose moose papoose recluse
        spruce truce vamoose
normal abnormal formal informal
north forth fourth henceforth
not apricot blot Camelot clot cot cybot dot forget-me-not forgot fought
        gavotte got hot hot-shot jot knot lot plot pot robot rot shot slingshot
        somewhat spot squat swat tot trot watt what yacht
notate rotate (see *ate*)
notch blotch botch crotch debauch hopscotch Scotch wristwatch
note afloat antidote bloat boat c-note coat connote denote dote float footnote
        gloat goat misquote moat oat overcoat promote quote remote riverboat
        rote smote throat tote turncoat underwrote vote wrote
notorious (see **us**)
novel grovel hovel
now allow avow bough bow brow chow cow disavow endow frau how
        kowtow ow plough plow row slough somehow sow thou vow wow
nude (see **feud**)
numb album aquarium auditorium become bum burdensome
        Christendom come cranium crematorium crumb curriculum dumb
        drum emporium fee-fi-fo-fum glum gum gymnasium hum
        kettledrum kingdom martyrdom maximum meddlesome medium
        millennium minimum mum museum opium overcome pendulum
        petroleum platinum plum premium quarrelsome radium random

n

rum sanitarium scum slum some strum succumb sum swum tedium thumb Tom Thumb Tweedledum uranium worrisome yum

number cucumber encumber lumber slumber umber

nurse adverse converse curse disburse disperse diverse hearse immerse intersperse inverse purse rehearse reverse terse transverse traverse universe verse worse

nursery anniversary cursory

nutty putty smutty

> Back then... there was no real outside force that made us write rhymes, because nobody was writing rhymes. So it was self-motivating. After a point, everyone started writing rhymes. My brother and I started writing rhymes and then everybody in our neighborhood who wanted to do the same thing that we was doing started writing. Then they became our inspiration. To crush them. And anytime we heard somebody say a rhyme that we thought was better, then that made us go back over over there and write something that was similar to that. So that if we ever went to battle that person, we'd have something like him, to crush him with.
>
> —Kid Creole, one of the first MCs with Grandmaster Flash
>
> (Yes, Yes, Y'all: Oral History of Hip-Hop's First Decade by Jim Fricke, Charlie Ahearn)

O

Oaktown brown clown crown down downtown drown frown gown hand-me-down lock-down noun renown town tumble-down upside down uptown

oath both growth loath overgrowth undergrowth

obey (see **say**)

object (see **defect**)

objection (see **rejection**)

obscenity amenity identity serenity

observe conserve curve deserve nerve preserve reserve serve swerve

occasion abrasion dissuasion equation evasion invasion persuasion

ocean commotion emotion locomotion lotion motion notion potion promotion

odd abroad applaud awed broad clod cod defraud façade fraud God guffawed Izod nod pod prod promenade quad rod roughshod shod sod squad trod wad

ode (see **road**)

odor exploder goader loader

of above dove glove ladylove love mourning dove shove turtle dove

off cough scoff trough

offensive apprehensive comprehensive defensive expensive extensive incomprehensive inexpensive intensive pensive

offer coffer cougher scoffer

often coffin coughin' soften

office abyss amiss analysis armistice bliss carcass cowardice 'dis dismiss emphasis gangstress hiss hypothesis kiss miss mistress nemesis prejudice Swiss synthesis this

ogle mogul

oh (see **so**)

oil broil coil foil loyal recoil royal spoil toil turmoil

old behold blindfold bold centerfold cold fold foothold foretold gold hold household marigold mold retold scold sold told uphold withhold

on Amazon autobahn Babylon bonbon Bonn brawn chiffon con Don dawn drawn echelon fawn gone lawn neon pawn pentagon silicon swan undergone upon wan woebegone wonton yawn

once bunts dunce fronts

one anyone begun bun comparison done everyone fun Galveston gun hon Hun jettison none nun oblivion outdone outrun over-done overrun phenomenon pun run shotgun shun simpleton skeleton son stun sun ton unison venison won

187 Devin Evan heaven Kevin seven leaven

only lonely

ooze blues booze bruise choose cruise lose news ooze snooze whose

opt adopt co-opt copped flopped mopped popped stopped

or (see **door**)

order boarder border disorder hoarder recorder

ordinary adversary airy arbitrary beneficiary berry bury canary capillary cautionary cherry commentary culinary customary dairy dictionary dietary dignitary disciplinary discretionary evolutionary extraordinary fairy February ferry functionary hairy hereditary honorary imaginary incendiary intermediary January Jerry legendary legionary literary luminary Mary mercenary military momentary monetary mortuary nary necessary obituary Perry planetary prairie proprietary pulmonary reactionary revolutionary sanctuary sanitary scary secretary seminary sherry solitary stationary temporary Terry very visionary vocabulary voluntary wary

Oreo Cleo geo Leo Rio trio

other another brother mother smother

ouch couch crouch grouch pouch slouch vouch

ounce announce bounce counts denounce mounts pounce pronounce renounce trounce

our devour flour hour scour (see *flower*)

out about boy scout blow-out bout clout devout doubt flout gout lout pout roundabout route scout shout snout spout sprout stout tout trout wash-out worn-out

outlaw Arkansas awe bra caw claw draw flaw gnaw guffaw hurrah jaw law Ma nah overdraw Pa paw raw saw seesaw shah slaw squaw straw thaw withdraw

outsider chider cider decider divider glider insider low-rider provider rider slider spider wider

oven lovin' shovin' sloven

over clover Dover drover moreover rover

overload a la mode abode bode code corrode episode erode explode forebode goad load lode mode mowed lode ode road rode sowed toad unload

overwhelm elm helm realm whelm
owe (see **blow**)
owl cowl foul fowl growl howl jowl prowl scowl waterfowl
own alone atone backbone baritone blown bone chaperone clone condone
cone cornerstone cyclone flown full-blown full-grown gramophone
grindstone groan grown headstone known k-tone loan lone
microphone milestone moan monotone mown overgrown
overthrown phone postpone prone saxophone sewn shown stone
telephone thrown tone trombone unknown xylophone zone
owner condoner donor groaner honer known 'er loan 'er loaner loner
moaner owner phone 'er toner
ox box chickenpox e-box equinox fox mailbox orthodox paradox
oxygen amen citizen den fen hen hydrogen men Ken pen regimen
specimen ten then yen Zen

O

" I'm a product of hip-hop. That's all I
listen to, what I grew up on besides what
my parents had going on in the house.
It's definitely hip-hop first and
everything else is just distant.
—Nelly "

P

Pacific hieroglyphic horrific prolific scientific specific terrific

pack almanac attack back black Cadillac cardiac clickety-clack crack
egomaniac feedback hack Hackensack haystack jack kleptomaniac
knack lack mack maniac plaque Pontiac Prozac quack rack sack
shack slack snack stack tack track whack yak zodiac

packet bracket jacket racket (see *it*)

packing backing cracking hacking lacking ransacking smacking
tracking whacking

pad ad add bad Brad cad Chad clad Dad egad fad glad grad had lad mad
nomad pad plaid sad shad Trinidad

paddle saddle straddle

page age cage gage rampage sage stage wage

paid aid arcade afraid barricade blade blockade braid brayed brigade
charade crusade degrade dismayed dissuade downgrade escapade
evade fade grade grenade hayed invade laid lemonade made maid
masquerade parade persuade played promenade raid renegade
serenade shade spade stockade suede tirade trade

pain abstain again airplane arraign ascertain attain brain Cain campaign
cane chain champagne cocaine complain contain crane detain
disdain domain drain entertain explain feign gain grain humane
hurricane hydroplane insane lane main Maine maintain mane
migraine obtain ordain pane pertain plain plane profane propane
rain refrain reign rein remain sane slain Spain sprain stain strain
sustain train vain vane vein wane windowpane

paint acquaint ain't complaint faint quaint restraint saint taint 'tain't

pair (see **air**)

pal canal chorale gal morale shall

palace Alice chalice Dallas malice phallus

panel channel flannel

panic (see **volcanic**)

paper caper draper escaper raper scraper shaper skyscraper taper vapor
(see *her*)

parachute (see **shoot**)

parade (see **afraid**)

paradise advice concise device dice entice ice lice mice nice precise price
rice sacrifice spice splice suffice thrice twice vice

parent apparent grandparent transparent (see *ant*)

park aardvark arc ark bark dark embark hark lark mark narc patriarch
remark shark spark stark

parlay (see **pay**)

parody (see **be**)

parole (see **roll**)

parrot carat carrot ferret merit tear it wear it (see *sit*)

parted broken-hearted carted charted chicken-hearted cold-hearted
darted departed fainthearted halfhearted hardhearted lion-hearted
smarted started

particle article nautical

party arty hearty smarty tarty

pass (see **class**)

passion ashen bashin' compassion fashion impassion

past aghast blast cast classed contrast fast flabbergast forecast gassed last
mast outlast overcast passed vast

pastor blaster caster castor disaster faster flabbergaster forecaster master
plaster postmaster taskmaster

patch attach batch catch detach dispatch hatch latch match scratch snatch

path aftermath bath homeopath math psychopath sociopath wrath

pathetic aesthetic alphabetic apathetic apologetic arithmetic athletic
cosmetic electromagnetic energetic frenetic genetic poetic
sympathetic synthetic theoretic

P

patrol (see **roll**)

pauper (see **proper**)

pause applause because cause clause claws gauze laws menopause Oz
paws Santa Claus was

pawn Amazon Babylon begone bonbon Bonn brawn chiffon con Don
dawn drawn fawn gone hexagon John lawn lexicon octagon on
Oregon pentagon silicon undergone upon withdrawn wanton yawn

pay AK array bay betray blue jay bouquet bray clay day decay delay disarray
dismay display Dr. Dre eh? essay exposé fray gay gray hay hey holiday
hooray José Kay lay matinee may moiré naysay negligée obey parlay
play portray protégé ray résumé ricochet risqué rosé say slay sleigh
soufflé stay stray sway they toupee way veejay weigh wordspray x-ray

peace cease crease decease decrease fleece geese grease Greece increase
lease masterpiece piece police release

peach beach breach each impeach leech peach preach reach screech speech teach

pearl curl earl girl hurl swirl twirl whirl

peck check Czech deck fleck heck neck Quebec speck trek wreck

pedal medal meddle peddle

peep barkeep cheep creep deep heap keep leap reap seep sheep sleep steep sweep weep

pen amen citizen den fen hen hydrogen Ken men oxygen regimen specimen ten then yen Zen

pencil prehensile stencil utensil

penny any Benny Jenny many

people Steeple (see *pull*)

perfect (see **defect**)

perfume assume consume costume exhume presume resume (see *room*)

perish bearish cherish

perjury surgery

perky Albuquerque murky quirky turkey

permission (see **tradition**)

persistent assistant consistent distant existent inconsistent insistent resistant subsistent

persuasive dissuasive evasive invasive pervasive

pervert (see **hurt**)

pest (see **best**)

pet alphabet bayonet bet brunette cabinet cadet cigarette clarinet cornet corvette debt duet forget fret gazette get jet Joliet Juliet let luncheonette marionette met net omelet pet quartet regret roulette set silhouette Somerset sunset sweat threat Tibet toilette upset vet 'vette violet wet yet

petty confetti fetti jetty machete spaghetti sweaty

p-funk bunk chunk clunk crunk cyberpunk drunk dunk flunk funk hunk junk monk p-funk plunk punk shrunk skunk slunk spunk stunk sunk trunk

phat at acrobat aristocrat autocrat bat brat bureaucrat cat chat democrat diplomat drat fat flat gat gnat hat mat pat phat rat rat-a-tat-tat sat scat spat stat thermostat vat

phone alone atone backbone baritone blown bone chaperone clone condone cone cornerstone cyclone flown full-blown full-grown

P

gramophone grindstone groan grown headstone known k-tone loan lone microphone milestone moan monotone mown overgrown overthrown own phone postpone prone saxophone sewn shown stone telephone thrown tone trombone unknown xylophone zone

phony acrimony alimony baloney bony crony macaroni matrimony patrimony pony sanctimony stony testimony Tony

photo De Soto koto roto Toto

pick arithmetic arsenic brick candlestick candlewick Catholic chick click copasetic flick heartsick hick kick lick limerick love-sick lunatic maverick medic music nick sick slick stick thick tic tick wick

picket cricket thicket ticket wicked wicket (see *it*)

pie (see **cry**)

piece cease crease decease decrease fleece geese grease Greece increase lease masterpiece peace police release

pierce fierce

pig big dig fig gig jig renege rig swig thingamajig twig underdig wig

pigeon religion widgeon

pile (see **smile**)

pillage tillage village

pillar caterpillar chiller distiller driller filler instiller killer shriller spiller swiller thriller tiller

pillow armadillo billow peccadillo willow

pimp blimp gimp limp shrimp skimp wimp

pimple dimple simple

pin (see **been**)

pinch cinch flinch inch lynch

pink blink brink chink clink drink fink ink kink link mink rink shrink sink slink stink wink zinc

pipe archetype gripe hype prototype ripe stereotype stripe swipe type wipe

pistol crystal

pitied prettied

pity city committee ditty gritty kitty pretty self-pity witty

pivot divot (see *it*)

place ace base bass brace case chase commonplace debase disgrace displace embrace encase erase face grace lace mace misplace pace race replace space steeplechase trace unlace vase

plague vague

P

plan an ban can can-can Dan fan Iran man Nan ran Tehran

plane (see **pain**)

planet gannet granite Janet pomegranate (see *it*)

plant ant aunt can't chant decant enchant grant implant rant scant shan't slant transplant

plastic bombastic drastic elastic enthusiastic fantastic gymnastic iconoclastic sarcastic scholastic spastic

plate (see **ate**)

platinum aluminum (see *scum*)

play (see **say**)

played (see **afraid**)

player betrayer conveyor grayer layer mayor payer portrayer prayer slayer soothsayer sprayer stayer surveyor

pleasant omnipresent peasant pheasant present

pleasure displeasure measure treasure

plenty twenty

plot (see **hot**)

plucked bucked chucked clucked ducked lucked mucked sucked trucked tucked

plummet summit (see *it*)

plump bump chump clump dump hump jump lump rump slump stump thump trump ump

plunge lunge sponge

plus (see **us**)

poem chrome chromosome comb dome foam gnome home honeycomb metronome Nome roam Rome tome

poetic aesthetic alphabetic apathetic apologetic arithmetic athletic cosmetic electromagnetic energetic frenetic genetic pathetic sympathetic synthetic theoretic

point anoint appoint counterpoint disappoint disjoint joint

pole (see **roll**)

police cease crease decease decrease fleece geese grease Greece increase lease masterpiece peace piece release

polish (see **abolish**)

politician (see **tradition**)

pollution (see **revolution**)

pond beyond blond bond correspond fond dawned respond spawned
vagabond wand yawned

ponder condor conned 'er fonder launder squander wander yonder

pony acrimony alimony baloney bony crony macaroni matrimony patrimony
phony sanctimony stony testimony Tony

pooch hooch mooch smooch

poodle boodle caboodle doodle feudal noodle Yankee Doodle

pool April fool cool drool fool ghoul Liverpool overrule rule school spool
stool tool whirlpool

poor amour boor contour detour moor paramour spoor tour (see *door*)

pop chop co-opt cop crop drop eavesdrop flop hip-hop hop lollipop mop
plop pop prop raindrop shop stop swap tip-top whop

pope (see **hope**)

po-po (see **so**)

porch scorch torch

portion abortion contortion distortion extortion proportion

posh (see **wash**)

post boast coast foremost furthermost ghost host innermost most roast
toast whipping post

postal annul coastal cull dull gull hull lull mull skull

pot apricot blot Camelot clot cot cybot dot forget-me-not forgot fought
gavotte got hot hot-shot jot knot lot not plot robot rot shot slingshot
somewhat spot squat swat tot trot watt what yacht

potion commotion emotion locomotion lotion motion notion
ocean promotion

pound (see **sound**)

pour (see **door**)

powder chowder louder prouder (see *her*)

power cauliflower cower deflower empower flower horsepower plower
shower tower (see *our*)

practical didactical tactical

prairie (see **ordinary**)

prank bank blank clank crank dank drank flank frank gank hank jank
outrank plank rank sank shank shrank spank stank tank thank yank

prayer (see *air*)

prayer betrayer conveyor grayer layer mayor payer player portrayer slayer
soothsayer sprayer stayer surveyor

preach beach breach each impeach leech peach reach screech
speech teach

preacher bleacher creature feature screecher teacher

precocious atrocious ferocious

present omnipresent peasant pheasant pleasant

president resident (see *bent*)

pressure fresher refresher thresher (see *sure*)

pretender (see **tender**)

pretentious conscientious contentious

pretty city committee ditty gritty kitty pity self-pity witty

price advice concise device dice entice ice lice mice nice paradise precise
rice sacrifice spice splice suffice thrice twice vice

pride beside bona fide bride collide confide countryside decide defied died
dignified divide eyed fireside guide hide hillside homicide inside lied
outside override provide reside ride side slide snide stride subdivide
subside suicide tide tried wide yuletide

priest beast ceased creased deceased east feast least pieced yeast

prime climb crime dime I'm lime pantomime rhyme slime show time
summertime thyme time

prince convince hints mints rinse since wince

print flint hint lint mint peppermint spearmint splint sprint squint tint

prior amplifier beautifier briar buyer crier cryer drier dryer flier friar higher
mystifier occupier simplifier slyer supplier testifier (see *fire*)

prison arisen risen wizen (see *in*)

privilege allege dredge edge fledge hedge ledge privilege sacrilege sledge wedge

prize (see **lies**)

probe disrobe globe Job robe strobe

produce (see **use**)

producer reducer seducer transducer (see *sir*)

profilin' beguilin' compilin' defilin' filin' juvenilin' pilin' revilin' rilin' stylin'

profit prophet (see *it*)

progressive aggressive depressive digressive excessive expressive
impressive possessive regressive successive

project Beck check Czech deck fleck heck neck peck Quebec speck
trek wreck

pronounce announce bounce counts denounce mounts ounce pounce
renounce trounce

P

proof aloof bulletproof goof hoof roof spoof waterproof weatherproof

proper bebopper bopper co-opter chopper copper cropper dropper eavesdropper eyedropper grasshopper hopper improper pauper pop-per sharecropper shopper stopper swapper teenybopper topper whopper (see *her*)

props cops chops co-opts crops flops hops lollipops mops raindrops stops swaps

prophet profit (see *it*)

prostitution (see **revolution**)

protect (see **defect**)

protester Chester contester fester investor jester Lester molester pester semester sequester tester Westchester Winchester

proud allowed aloud cloud crowd enshroud loud plowed shroud thundercloud

prove approve behoove disapprove disprove groove improve move remove

provoke (see **joke**)

prude brood clued conclude crude dude exclude food glued include intrude misconstrued mood preclude rude seclude shrewd wooed

psalm aplomb bomb calm embalm Guam Mom palm qualm

psychosis diagnosis narcosis neurosis prognosis psychosis

pub Beelzebub bub club cub grub hub hubbub rub rub-a-dub-dub scrub shrub snub stub sub tub

pucker bucker chucker clucker sapsucker seersucker sucker trucker (see *her*)

puddle cuddle fuddle huddle muddle

puke duke juke uke

pull bull cock-and-bull do-able full marble wool (see *beautiful*)

pulse convulse impulse repulse

pumpkin bumpkin

punch brunch bunch crunch hunch lunch munch scrunch

puncture acupuncture conjuncture juncture

punk bunk chunk clunk crunk cyberpunk drunk dunk flunk funk hunk junk monk p-funk plunk shrunk skunk slunk spunk stunk sunk trunk

punt affront blunt brunt bunt confront forefront front grunt hunt runt shunt stunt

pup buttercup cup fed up hard-up pick-up pup suckup sup up

pupil scruple

P

puppy guppy yuppie

pure allure armature assure brochure caricature cocksure cure demure
endure ensure expenditure forfeiture immature impure insecure
insure liqueur literature lure manicure mature miniature obscure
overture pedicure premature reassure secure signature sure tablature
temperature your

purge (see **verge**)

push bush cush

put afoot foot lead foot pussyfoot tenderfoot

puzzler guzzler

PWT (see **be**)

> As far as the writing process goes, I
> write anywhere. Most of the time I just go
> into the studio, they play the track and I
> write right there. Or I'll go home and
> write. My kids is getting chicken grease
> on the paper while I'm writing, and they're
> running in and out and I'm still [writing].
> I don't have any particular process, I just
> love to write rhymes. At my house I've got
> literally two big suitcases of that old,
> grandma luggage, the old luggage full of
> papers and rhymes from years ago that
> I've never used. Writing's something I
> really enjoy.
>
> —LL Cool J

P

q

QB (see **be**)

quaint acquaint ain't complaint faint paint restraint saint taint 'tain't

quake ache bake brake break cake fake flake forsake headache heartache
  keepsake make mistake opaque rake shake snake stake steak take
  wake

quality (see **be**)

qualm aplomb bomb calm embalm Guam Mom palm psalm

quart abort assort comfort contort court deport distort escort exhort export
  extort fort import passport port report resort retort short snort sort
  sport support thwart tort transport wart

queen bean between caffeine canteen chlorine clean codeine Colleen
  convene cuisine dean demean evergreen Florentine foreseen
  gasoline Gene green guillotine Halloween in-between intervene
  kerosene lean lien machine marine mean mezzanine Nazarene
  nectarine nicotine obscene preen quarantine ravine routine sardine
  scene seen serene spleen submarine tambourine tangerine teen
  thirteen (etc.) Vaseline velveteen wintergreen wolverine

queer (see **near**)

quench bench clench drench French monkey wrench stench trench wench
  wrench

quest arrest attest best breast chest congest crest detest digest divest
  double-breast infest ingest interest invest jest manifest molest nest
  protest request rest single-breast suggest test vest

quibble dribble kibble nibble scribble sibyl

quicken chicken sicken stricken thicken (see *in*)

quickly prickly sickly slickly thickly

quiet diet riot (see *it*)

quip battleship chip clip dip drip equip flip grip gyp hip lip nip rip scrip ship
  slip snip strip tip trip whip zip

quirk clerk handiwork irk jerk Kirk lurk murk overwork perk quirk smirk
  Turk work

quirky Albuquerque murky perky turkey

quit befit bit fit 'git grit kit knit hit it jit legit lit mitt nit-wit pit sit twit unfit
  ultimate wit zit

quite appetite bite blight bright byte contrite copyright daylight delight
  despite dynamite excite Fahrenheit fight flight fright headlight height

ignite invite kite knight light midnight might moonlight night outright parasite plight polite recite reunite right satellite sight site sleight slight spite starlight sunlight tight trite twilight unite white write

quitter counterfeiter critter fitter fritter glitter litter sitter transmitter twitter (see *her*)

quiz biz fizz frizz his is showbiz 'tis whiz

quota Dakota iota Minnesota

quote afloat antidote bloat boat c-note coat connote denote dote float footnote gloat goat misquote moat note oat overcoat promote remote riverboat rote smote throat tote turncoat underwrote vote wrote

Rap continues to be popular among today's urban youth for the same reasons it was a draw in the early days: It is still an accessible form of self-expression capable of eliciting positive affirmation from one's peers. Because rap has evolved to become such a big business, it has given many the false illusion of being a quick escape from the harshness of inner city life. There are many kids out there under the belief that all they need to do is write a few "fresh" rhymes and they're off to the good life.

—Dave, D, hip-hop journalist, historian, DJ

r

rabble babble dabble scrabble

racial facial glacial spatial

racket bracket jacket packet (see *it*)

radar A&R are bar bazaar bizarre car caviar cigar czar disbar far guitar jar par radar scar spar star tar

rag bag brag do-rag drag flag gag hag lag mag nag sag shag slag snag stag swag tag wag

ragamuffin buffin' muffin puffin ragamuffin stuffin' toughen

raging aging caging gauging paging staging waging

raid (see **afraid**)

rail (see **ale**)

rain abstain again airplane arraign ascertain attain brain Cain campaign cane chain champagne cocaine complain contain crane detain disdain domain drain entertain explain feign gain grain humane hurricane hydroplane insane lane main Maine maintain mane migraine obtain ordain pain pane pertain plain plane profane propane refrain reign rein remain sane slain Spain sprain stain strain sustain train vain vane vein wane windowpane

rainbow (see **blow**)

raindrop chop co-opt cop crop drop eavesdrop flop hip-hop hop lollipop mop plop pop prop shop stop swap tip-top whop

rainy brainy grainy zany

ramble amble gamble scramble shamble

ran an ban can can-can Dan fan Iran Koran man Nan plan Tehran

ranch avalanche branch

range arrange change derange estrange exchange strange

rank bank blank clank crank dank drank flank frank gank Hank jank outrank plank prank sank shank shrank skank spank stank tank thank yank

rant (see **ant**)

rap cap chap clap dap flap gap handicap lap map mishap nap sap scrap slap snap strap tap trap wrap zap

rape ape cape cityscape drape escape grape landscape seascape shape tape

rapper capper clapper dapper flapper handicapper slapper snapper tapper whippersnapper wiretapper wrapper yapper

raptor actor benefactor contractor detractor distracter extractor factor
        reactor refractor tractor

rapture capture recapture (see *your*)

rare (see **air**)

Rastafarian Aquarian Aryan barbarian buryin' Cesarean disciplinarian
        ferryin' humanitarian libertarian librarian Marion marryin' Sagittarian
        Unitarian vegetarian veterinarian

rat at acrobat aristocrat autocrat bat brat bureaucrat cat chat democrat
        diplomat drat fat flat gat gnat hat mat pat phat rat-a-tat-tat sat scat
        spat stat thermostat vat

rate (see **ate**)

rational international irrational national passional

rattle battle cattle chattel embattle prattle Seattle tattle

ravage average cabbage savage

raw Arkansas awe bra caw claw draw flaw gnaw guffaw hurrah jaw law
        Ma nah outlaw overdraw Pa paw saw seesaw shah slaw squaw straw
        thaw withdraw

razor appraiser blazer gazer laser maser phaser praiser stargazer

reach beach breach each impeach leech peach preach screech
        speech teach

react (see **act**)

reaction (see **action**)

read agreed breed centipede concede creed deed exceed feed greed heed
        inbreed knead lead mislead need precede proceed recede secede
        seed speed stampede succeed Swede tweed weed

read ahead bed bedspread bread bred coed dead dread fed figurehead
        fled flowerbed fountainhead gingerbread head inbred lead led
        misled misread overfed red riverbed said shed shred sled sped
        spread thoroughbred thread underfed unthread wed

R

realm elm helm overwhelm whelm

rear (see **near**)

reason pleasin' season sneezin' squeezin' teasin' wheezin' (see *son*)

receipt (see **meet**)

receive achieve believe bereave conceive disbelieve eve grieve heave
        leave receive relieve reprieve retrieve sleeve weave

recent decent indecent

recital entitle title vital

recognition (see **tradition**)
recognize advertise advise analyze apologize arise authorize baptize
capitalize capsize characterize comprise compromise criticize demise
deputize despise devise dies disguise economize emphasize
enterprise epitomize eulogize excise exercise exorcise eyes
familiarize fertilize flies generalize hypnotize idealize idolize
immortalize improvise italicize legalize lies materialize memorize
merchandise minimize neutralize ostracize paralyze patronize
penalize personalize philosophize plagiarize prize rationalize realize
recognize reprise revise rise satirize scandalize scrutinize size
socialize specialize spies sterilize stigmatize subsidize summarize
sunrise supervise surmise surprise sympathize terrorize theorize
thighs ties tranquilize utilize verbalize visualize vocalize wise
red (see **said**)
redemption exemption preemption
refinery binary finery
reflection (see **rejection**)
reflex BMX complex decks duplex DMX ex flex hex Lex necks pecks
Rolodex sex specs Tex unisex
region collegian Norwegian
regret alphabet bayonet bet brunette cabinet cadet cigarette clarinet cornet
corvette debt duet epithet etiquette forget fret gazette get jet Joliet
Juliet let luncheonette marionette met net omelet pet quartet
roulette set silhouette Somerset sunset sweat threat Tibet toilette
upset vet 'vette violet wet yet
reject (see **defect**)
rejection affection bisection circumspection collection complexion
connection correction defection deflection detection direction
disaffection dissection ejection election erection imperfection
infection inflection inspection intersection introspection objection
perfection projection protection reflection resurrection retrospection
section selection vivisection
relax ax backs fax jacks lax max packs Saks sax slacks tax wax
release cease crease decease decrease fleece geese grease Greece
increase lease masterpiece peace piece police
reliance alliance appliance compliance defiance reliance
religion pigeon widgeon
remain (see **rain**)

R

remark aardvark arc ark bark dark embark hark lark mark narc park
    patriarch shark spark stark

remember December dismember ember member November September

reminiscing dismissing 'dissing hissing kissing missing

remorse coarse course divorce endorse force horse Norse reinforce
    resource source

remove approve behoove disapprove disprove groove improve
    move prove

Reno andantino bambino Filipino keno

rent (see **bent**)

rental accidental coincidental complemental compliment continental dental
    departmental detrimental experimental fundamental gentle governmental
    incidental intercontinental lentil mental monumental Oriental parental
    regimental rudimental sentimental supplemental temperamental

repair (see **air**)

repeat (see **meet**)

resemble assemble dissemble tremble (see *bull*)

resident president (see *bent*)

resisted assisted enlisted existed fisted insisted listed misted persisted
    subsisted twisted

respect (see **defect**)

rest arrest attest best blessed breast Bucharest Budapest chest congest
    contest crest detest digest divest dressed guessed guest infest ingest
    interest invest jest manifest messed molest nest pest protest request
    second-best suggest test unrest vest zest

result adult catapult consult cult difficult exult insult occult

retire (see **fire**)

return adjourn burn churn concern discern earn fern intern kern learn
    overturn sojourn spurn stern taciturn turn urn yearn

reveal (see **steal**)

revenge avenge Stonehenge

revolt bolt colt dolt jolt thunderbolt

revolution absolution attribution constitution contribution destitution
    dilution dissolution distribution electrocution evolution execution
    institution pollution prosecution prostitution resolution retribution
    solution substitution

revolve absolve devolve dissolve evolve involve solve

R

revolver solver

reward aboard accord afford award board bored ford harpsichord hoard lord overboard poured shuffleboard soared sword ward

rhyme chime climb crime dime I'm lime mime pantomime prime slime show time summertime thyme time

rib ad lib crib fib glib rib

rich bewitch bitch ditch enrich glitch hitch pitch snitch stitch switch twitch which

rid bid did forbid grid hid invalid lid Madrid pyramid skid slid squid

riddle diddle fiddle griddle middle twiddle

ride beside bona fide bride collide confide countryside decide defied died dignified divide eyed fireside guide hide hillside homicide inside lied outside override pride provide reside ride side slide snide stride subdivide subside suicide tide tried wide yuletide

ridge abridge bridge fridge

ridicule molecule mule ridicule vestibule Yule

rifle Eiffel eyeful rifle stifle trifle

rigid frigid

ring anything bling-bling bring cling ding evening everything fling jing king sing sling spring sting string swing thing wing wring (add "-ing" to action words, e.g., run[ning], etc.)

riot diet quiet (see *it*)

R.I.P. (see *be*)

rip (see *trip*)

ripe archetype gripe hype pipe prototype stereotype stripe swipe type wipe

ripple cripple nipple triple

rise (see **lies**)

risen arisen prison risen wizen (see *in*)

rising advertising advising agonizing analyzing apologizing appetizing baptizing compromising criticizing despising devising disguising equalizing eulogizing evangelizing exercising generalizing harmonizing improvising jeopardizing memorizing mesmerizing minimizing modernizing organizing patronizing plagiarizing prizing realizing recognizing revising scrutinizing sizing sterilizing subsidizing supervising surmising surprising sympathizing tantalizing terrorizing uprising utilizing visualizing vocalizing

risk asterisk brisk disk frisk whisk

risky frisky whiskey

rival arrival revival survival

river deliver giver liver quiver shiver sliver (see *her*)

rizzi busy dizzy frizzy Lizzie Tin Lizzie tizzy

roach approach broach coach cockroach encroach poach reproach

road a la mode abode bode code corrode episode erode explode forebode goad load lode mode mowed lode ode overload rode sowed toad unload

roam chrome chromosome comb dome foam gnome home honeycomb metronome Nome poem Rome tome

rob blob bob cob fob gob hob hobnob job knob lob mob nob slob snob sob swab throb

robber clobber dauber jobber slobber swabber

robe disrobe globe Job probe strobe

robust (see **trust**)

rock Bangkok beanstalk boondock clock cock cornstalk crock deadlock defrock dock dreadlock flintlock flock frock gawk glock gridlock hawk hock J. S. Bach jock knock Little Rock livestock lock mock Mohawk padlock peacock shock sidewalk small talk smock sock squawk stalk stock talk tomahawk unlock walk wok

rocker balker blocker Knickerbocker knocker locker mocker shocker soccer stalker talker walker (see *her*)

rocket docket hocket locket pocket socket sprocket (see *it*)

rod abroad applaud awed broad clod cod defraud façade fraud God guffawed Izod nod odd pod prod promenade quad roughshod shod sod squad trod wad

rode (see **road**)

roll bowl buttonhole cajole casserole coal control dole droll enroll goal hole loophole Maypole mole Old King Cole oriole parole patrol pole poll porthole role scroll tadpole toll troll whole

roller bowler consoler controller molar polar solar stroller troller

rollo bolo dolo gigolo piccolo polo solo tremolo

romance advance ants chance circumstance dance enhance extravagance finance France glance lance pants prance stance trance

romantic antic Atlantic chromatic frantic gigantic pedantic transatlantic

roof aloof bulletproof goof hoof proof spoof waterproof weatherproof

rookie bookie cooky hooky lookee

R

room bloom boom broom cloakroom doom entomb flume gloom groom
    tomb whom womb zoom

roost boost

rooster booster (see *her*)

root (see **shoot**)

rope antelope cantaloupe cope dope elope envelope grope gyroscope
    hope horoscope kaleidoscope microscope mope pope scope slope
    soap stethoscope telescope

Rosco (see *so*)

rose arose chose close compose decompose depose disclose dispose
    doze enclose expose foreclose froze goes hose impose indispose
    knows nose owes pose predispose presuppose prose suppose those
    toes transpose woes

rosy cozy dozy mosey posy

rotate notate (see *ate*)

rotten begotten cotton gotten forgotten

rough bluff buff cuff duff enough fluff gruff huff muff powder puff scruff
    scuff snuff stuff tough

rougher bluffer buffer duffer gruffer puffer suffer tougher

round abound around astound background battleground bloodhound
    bound compound confound downed dumbfound found ground
    hound impound merry-go-round mound pound profound renowned
    resound sound spellbound surround under-ground wound

roar (see **door**)

routine (see **mean**)

row (see **blow**)

R

rowdy cloudy cum laude dowdy howdy

royal broil coil foil loyal oil recoil spoil toil turmoil

royalty loyalty (see *be*)

rub Beelzebub bub club cub grub hub hubbub pub rub-a-dub-dub scrub
    shrub snub stub sub tub

ruby booby

rudder shudder udder

rude brood clued conclude crude dude exclude food glued include intrude
    misconstrued mood preclude prude seclude shrewd wooed

rule April fool cool drool fool ghoul Liverpool overrule pool school spool
    stool tool whirlpool

ruler cooler drooler

rum (see **dumb**)

rumor bloomer boomer consumer humor tumor

run anyone begun bun comparison done everyone fun Galveston gun hon Hun jettison none nun oblivion one outdone outrun overdone overrun phenomenon pun shotgun shun simpleton skeleton son stun sun ton unison venison won

Run DMC (see **be**)

rung (see **young**)

runner gunner stunner

rural extramural intramural mural neural plural

rush blush brush crush flush gush lush mush plush slush thrush underbrush

rust adjust August bust crust dust disgust distrust encrust entrust gust just lust mistrust must robust thrust trust unjust

> [Rap] has become lifestyle. We've brought all these races together in dialogue. The CNN of the hip-hop generation, as Chuck D referred to it years ago, was at that point the CNN of the young Black community...but now its [audience is] 80% non-Black. Not many people in hip-hop realize that they are more powerful than the politicians.
>
> —Russell Simmons
>
> DefJam Records Founder

R

S

sack almanac attack back black Cadillac cardiac clickety-clack crack egomaniac feedback hack Hackensack haystack jack kleptomaniac knack lack mack maniac pack plaque Pontiac Prozac quack rack sack shack slack snack stack tack track whack yak zodiac

sacrifice advice concise device dice entice ice lice mice nice paradise precise price rice spice splice suffice thrice twice vice

sad ad add bad Brad cad Chad clad Dad egad fad glad grad had lad mad nomad pad plaid shad Trinidad

sag bag brag do-rag drag flag gag hag lag mag nag rag shag slag snag stag swag tag wag

said ahead bed bedspread bread bred coed dead dread fed figurehead fled flowerbed fountainhead gingerbread head inbred lead led misled misread overfed read red riverbed shed shred sled sped spread thoroughbred thread underfed unthread wed

sail (see **ale**)

sailor inhaler jailer sailor staler trailer wailer whaler

saint acquaint ain't complaint faint paint quaint restraint taint 'tain't

salary calorie gallery Mallory

saloon (see **moon**)

salt assault cobalt exalt fault halt malt somersault vault

same acclaim aim became blame came claim exclaim fame flame frame game inflame lame maim name proclaim shame tame

sample ample example trample

sand and band brand canned command contraband demand expand fanned grand hand land panned planned reprimand Rio Grande stand

sandal candle dandle handle scandal vandal

sandy Andy brandy candy dandy handy randy

sang bang boomerang clang dang fang gang-bang hang orangutan rang slang sprang

sanity Christianity humanity insanity profanity vanity

sank bank blank clank crank dank drank flank frank gank Hank jank outrank plank prank rank shank shrank skank spank stank tank thank yank

sappy crappie happy nappy pappy scrappy slaphappy yappy

sarcasm bioplasm chasm enthusiasm plasm spasm

sarcastic bombastic drastic elastic enthusiastic fantastic gymnastic iconoclastic plastic scholastic spastic

sat (see **at**)

satisfactory factory refractory (see *story*)

savage ravage

save behave brave cave concave crave engrave forgave gave grave knave pave rave shave slave waive wave

savior behavior misbehavior

saw Arkansas awe bra caw claw draw flaw gnaw guffaw hurrah jaw law Ma nah outlaw overdraw Pa paw raw seesaw shah slaw squaw straw thaw withdraw

say AK array bay betray blue jay bouquet bray clay day decay delay disarray dismay display Dr. Dre eh? essay exposé fray gay gray hay hey holiday hooray José Kay lay matinee may moiré naysay negligée obey parlay pay play portray protégé ray résumé ricochet risqué rosé slay sleigh soufflé stay stray sway they toupee way veejay weigh wordspray x-ray

scald appalled bald

scandal candle dandle handle sandal vandal

scanky cranky hanky hanky-panky lanky Yankee

scare (see **air**)

scarf barf snarf

scrap cap chap clap dap flap gap handicap lap map mishap nap rap sap slap snap strap tap trap wrap zap

scary adversary airy arbitrary beneficiary berry bury canary capillary cautionary cherry commentary culinary customary dairy dictionary dietary dignitary disciplinary discretionary evolutionary extraordinary fairy February ferry functionary hairy hereditary honorary imaginary incendiary intermediary January Jerry legendary legionary literary luminary Mary mercenary military momentary monetary mortuary nary necessary obituary ordinary Perry planetary prairie proprietary pulmonary reactionary revolutionary sanctuary sanitary secretary seminary sherry solitary stationary temporary Terry very visionary vocabulary voluntary wary

scrazy crazy daisy foogazy hazy lazy

scribe bribe circumscribe describe jibe prescribe subscribe tribe vibe

scene (see **seen**)

scenery beanery greenery machinery

scent absent accent augment cement comment compliment consent content dent dissent ferment frequent indent invent present prevent relent rent repent represent resent supplement tent torment vent

school April fool cool drool fool ghoul Liverpool overrule pool rule spool stool tool whirlpool

scientific hieroglyphic horrific pacific prolific specific terrific

scope (see **hope**)

score (see **door**)

scorn adorn airborne born Cape Horn Capricorn corn forlorn horn lovelorn Matterhorn morn mourn popcorn stillborn sworn unicorn warn worn

scout about Boy Scout blow-out bout clout devout doubt flout gout lout out pout roundabout route shout snout spout sprout stout tout trout wash-out worn-out

scramble amble gamble ramble shamble

scratch attach batch catch detach dispatch hatch latch match patch snatch

scream beam cream deem dream esteem extreme gleam ream regime scheme seam seen steam stream supreme team teem

screw (see **do**)

screwy chewy dewy Drambuie gluey gooey hooey Louie phooey St. Louie

script chipped dipped crypt equipped manuscript sipped transcript whipped zipped

scrub Beelzebub bub club cub grub hub hubbub pub rub rub-a-dub-dub shrub snub stub sub tub

scruple pupil

scuba Cuba tuba

scuffle duffle muffle ruffle shuffle truffle

scum album aquarium auditorium become bum burdensome Christendom come cranium crematorium crumb curriculum drum dump emporium fee-fi-fo-fum glum gum gymnasium hum kettledrum kingdom martyrdom maximum meddlesome medium millennium minimum mum museum numb opium overcome pendulum petroleum platinum plum premium quarrel-some radium random rum sanitarium slum some strum succumb sum swum tedium thumb Tom Thumb Tweedledum uranium worrisome yum

sea (see **be**)

seal (see **steal**)

search besmirch birch church lurch perch research search smirch

season pleasin' reason sneezin' squeezin' teasin' wheezin' (see *son*)

seat (see **sweet**)

secure (see **pure**)

seduce abuse accuse confuse cues deduce diffuse disuse duce excuse induce infuse introduce juice misuse obtuse peruse produce profuse reduce refuse reproduce Syracuse use

see (see **be**)

seed agreed breed centipede concede creed deed exceed feed greed heed inbreed knead lead mislead need precede proceed read recede reed secede speed stampede succeed Swede tweed weed

seeing agreeing being decreeing disagreeing farseeing fleeing foreseeing freeing guaranteeing overseeing teeing unseeing

seek beak bleak creek eek freak geek leak meek reek speak tweak weak week

seen bean between caffeine canteen chlorine clean codeine Colleen convene cuisine dean demean evergreen Florentine foreseen gasoline Gene green guillotine Halloween in-between intervene kerosene lean lien machine marine mean mezzanine Nazarene nectarine nicotine obscene preen quarantine queen ravine routine sardine scene serene spleen submarine tambourine tangerine teen thirteen (etc.) Vaseline velveteen wintergreen wolverine

self elf herself himself itself myself shelf yourself

sell bell belle Carmel carrousel cell clientele dell dwell excel farewell fell gel hell hotel infidel knell mademoiselle personnel shell smell spell tell well yell

selling compelling dwelling excelling expelling foretelling fortune-telling misspelling quelling rebelling repelling shelling smelling spelling swelling telling underselling yelling

semester Chester contester fester investor jester Lester molester pester protester sequester tester Westchester Winchester

send apprehend ascend attend befriend bend blend commend comprehend condescend defend depend descend dividend end expend extend fend friend intend lend mend offend penned pretend recommend spend suspend tend transcend trend unbend

sensational congregational creational educational inspirational recreational representational

sense (see **fence**)

sensed against condensed fenced

senses commences defenses dispenses fences offenses tenses
sensing condensing dispensing fencing incensing recompensing
sent (see **bent**)
sentence repentance
sequel equal
serenity amenity obscenity
serial cereal immaterial material managerial ministerial
serious (see **us**)
sermon determine German merman vermin
serve conserve curve deserve nerve observe preserve reserve swerve
settle kettle metal mettle petal resettle settle
730 dirty flirty thirty
severe (see **near**)
sewer bluer brewer doer fewer interviewer newer pursuer reviewer skewer
        truer viewer wooer
sex BMX complex decks duplex DMX ex flex hex Lex necks pecks reflex
        Rolodex specs Tex unisex
shack (see **sack**)
shackle cackle crackle hackle ramshackle tackle
shade (see **afraid**)
shake ache bake brake break cake fake flake forsake headache heartache keepsake
        make mistake opaque quake rake sake snake stake steak take wake
shall canal chorale gal morale pal
shallow callow fallow hallow mallow marshmallow tallow
sham (see **am**)
shamble amble gamble ramble scramble
shame acclaim aim became blame came claim exclaim fame flame frame
        game inflame lame maim name proclaim same tame
shank (see **shank**)
shanty aunty panty scanty
shape (see **ape**)
shark aardvark arc ark bark dark embark hark lark mark narc park patriarch
        remark spark stark
sharp carp harp
she (see **be**)
shelf elf herself himself itself myself self yourself

S

shelter belter smelter swelter

shield battlefield Chesterfield field wield yield

shift drift gift lift spendthrift swift thrift

shifty fifty nifty thrifty

shine align asinine assign benign combine concubine confine consign decline define design dine divine entwine fine incline line malign mine nine outshine pine porcupine recline refine resign Rhine shrine sign spine stein swine twine underline undermine vine whine wine

ship (see **trip**)

shirt alert avert blurt concert convert curt curtain desert dessert dirt divert exert expert extrovert flirt hurt insert introvert invert pervert skirt squirt subvert yogurt

shock Bangkok beanstalk boondock clock cock cornstalk crock deadlock defrock dock dreadlock flintlock flock frock gawk glock gridlock hawk hock J. S. Bach jock knock Little Rock livestock lock mock Mohawk padlock peacock rock sidewalk small talk Tupoc smock sock squawk stalk stock talk tomahawk unlock walk wok

shoe (see **do**)

shoot absolute acute astute attribute beaut boot brute Butte chute commute compute constitute coot cute destitute dilute dispute disrepute dissolute electrocute en route execute flute fruit hoot loot lute minute moot mute newt parachute persecute pollute prosecute prostitute pursuit recruit refute repute resolute root route scoot snoot substitute suit toot transmute uproot

shop (see **drop**)

short abort assort comfort contort court deport distort escort exhort export extort fort import passport port quart report resort retort short snort sort sport support thwart tort transport wart

shot apricot blot Camelot clot cot cybot dot forget-me-not forgot fought gavotte got hot hot-shot jot knot lot not plot pot robot rot slingshot somewhat spot squat swat tot trot watt what yacht

shotgun (see **son**)

should brotherhood could fatherhood firewood good Hollyhood Hollywood hood likelihood livelihood misunderstood motherhood neighborhood sisterhood stood understood withstood womanhood wood would

shout about Boy Scout blow-out bout clout devout doubt flout gout lout pout roundabout route scout snout spout sprout stout tout trout wash-out worn-out

S

shove above dove glove ladylove love mourning dove of turtle dove
show blow afro although banjo beau below bestow bow buffalo
bungalow calico crossbow crow depot doe domino dough
embryo escrow Eskimo flow foe forgo fro gazebo gigolo glow go
grow heigh-ho ho-ho hobo hoe incognito indigo Joe know long
ago low Mexico mistletoe mow no oboe oh outgrow overflow
overgrow overthrow owe Pinocchio plateau quo rainbow ratio roe
row sew slow snow so Soho status quo stow studio though throw
tiptoe to-and-fro toe Tokyo tow tremolo undergo undertow vertigo
woe yo yo-yo
shower cauliflower cower deflower empower flower horsepower plower
power tower (see *our*)
shown (see **stone**)
showtime (see **slime**)
shrank bank blank clank crank dank drank flank frank gank Hank jank
outrank plank prank rank sank shank skank spank stank tank
thank yank
shrewd brood clued conclude crude dude exclude food glued include
intrude misconstrued mood preclude prude rude seclude wooed
shrewdly crudely lewdly rudely
shrimp blimp gimp limp pimp skimp wimp
shrine (see **fine**)
shrink blink brink chink clink drink fink ink kink link mink pink rink sink slink
stink wink zinc
shroud allowed aloud cloud crowd enshroud loud plowed proud
thundercloud
shuffle duffle muffle ruffle truffle
shut but butt coconut cut glut gut halibut hut King Tut mutt nut putt rut
scuttlebutt slut smut strut uncut
shy (see **cry**)
shyly dryly highly Reilly slyly spryly wily wryly
sick arithmetic arsenic brick candlestick candlewick Catholic chick click
copasetic flick heartsick hick kick lick limerick love-sick lunatic
maverick medic nick pick slick stick thick tic tick wick
side beside bona fide bride collide confide countryside decide defied died
dignified divide eyed fireside guide hide hillside homicide inside lied
outside override pride provide reside ride slide snide stride subdivide
subside suicide tide tried wide yuletide

sight appetite bite blight bright byte contrite copyright daylight delight despite dynamite excite Fahrenheit fight flight fright headlight height ignite invite kite knight light midnight might moonlight night outright parasite plight polite quite recite reunite right satellite site sleight slight spite starlight sunlight tight trite twilight unite white write

sign align asinine assign benign combine concubine confine consign decline define design dine divine entwine fine incline line malign mine nine outshine pine porcupine recline refine resign Rhine shine shrine spine stein swine twine underline undermine vine whine wine

signature (see **pure**)

signify dignify (see *cry*)

silk bilk ilk milk

silly Billy Chile Chili chilly dilly filly frilly hillbilly hilly lily Philly Piccadilly piccalilli shrilly willy-nilly

simmer dimmer glimmer grimmer primmer skimmer slimmer swimmer trimmer

simple dimple pimple

sin aspirin been begin Benjamin Berlin bin chagrin chin Crooklyn discipline feminine fin 5x10 genuine gin grin heroine in inn kin mandolin mannequin masculine moccasin origin pin saccharine shin skin spin thick-and-thin thin tin twin violin within win

since convince hints mints prince rinse wince

sincere (see **near**)

sincerity austerity dexterity insincerity posterity prosperity severity

sing anything bring cling ding evening everything fling king ring sling spring sting string swing thing wing wring (add "-ing" to action words, e.g., run[ning], etc.)

single intermingle jingle Kris Kringle mingle shingle tingle

sink blink brink chink clink drink fink ink kink link mink pink rink shrink slink stink think wink zinc

sinner B.F. Skinner beginner breadwinner dinner inner skinner spinner thinner winner

sinister administer minister

sir (see **her**)

sirloin purloin

sister assister blister mister resister twister (see *her*)

sit befit bit fit 'git grit kit knit hit it jit legit lit mitt nit-wit pit quit twit unfit ultimate wit zit

5

size (see **lies**)

sizzle chisel drizzle fizzle frizzle grizzle swizzle

skank (see **shrank**)

skate (see **ate**)

skeptic antiseptic septic

sketch catch etch fetch kvetch retch stretch wretch

skid bid did forbid grid hid invalid lid Madrid pyramid rid slid squid

skin (see **been**)

skinny New Guinea ninny tinny

skirt (see **shirt**)

skull annul cull dull gull hull lull mull scull

skunk bunk chunk clunk crunk cyberpunk drunk dunk flunk funk hunk junk
    monk p-funk plunk punk shrunk slunk spunk stunk sunk trunk

sky (see **cry**)

skyscraper caper draper escaper paper raper scraper shaper taper

slab blab cab crab dab drab fab gab grab jab lab nab scab stab tab

slacker attacker backer blacker cracker hacker hijacker nutcracker packer
    ransacker smacker tracker

slam (see **am**)

slang bang boomerang clang dang fang gang-bang hang orangutan rang
    sang sprang

slant (see **ant**)

slap cap chap clap dap flap gap handicap lap map mishap nap rap sap
    scrap snap strap tap trap wrap zap

slaughter blotter daughter hotter otter plotter spotter squatter trotter water

slave behave brave cave concave crave engrave forgave gave grave knave
    pave rave save shave waive wave

slavery (see **be**)

sleaze (see **ease**)

sled (see **said**)

sleep barkeep cheep creep deep heap keep leap peep reap seep sheep
    steep sweep weep

sleeve achieve believe bereave conceive disbelieve eve grieve heave leave
    perceive receive relieve reprieve retrieve weave

sleigh (see **say**)

slept accept adept crept except intercept kept overslept stepped swept wept

sleuth booth couth Duluth tooth truth uncouth youth

slid bid did forbid grid hid invalid lid Madrid pyramid rid skid squid

slim brim dim Eminem grim gym hymn limb pseudonym skim swim trim whim

slime chime climb crime dime I'm lime mime pantomime prime rhyme show time summertime thyme time

slob blob bob cob fob gob hob hobnob job knob lob mob nob rob snob sob swab throb

sloppy choppy copy floppy hoppy poppy soppy

slow (see **blow**)

slum (see **scum**)

slumber cucumber cumber encumber lumber number umber

slut (see **but**)

small all ball bawl brawl call crawl doll drawl fall gall haul install mall maul Montreal nightfall overhaul parasol pitfall protocol rainfall scrawl shawl snowfall sprawl stall tall thrall wall waterfall y'all

smart apart art cart chart counterpart dart depart heart mart part start sweetheart tart upstart

smash ash balderdash bash brash cash clash crash dash flash gash gnash rash rehash slash splash stash thrash trash

smell bell belle Carmel carrousel cell clientele dell dwell excel farewell fell gel hell hotel infidel knell mademoiselle personnel sell shell spell tell well yell

smile aisle awhile beguile bile compile crocodile defile file isle juvenile meanwhile mile Nile pile rile style tile vile while wile worthwhile

smiling beguiling compiling defiling filing piling reconciling reviling styling tiling

smirk clerk handiwork irk jerk Kirk lurk murk overwork perk quirk shirk Turk work

smoke (see **joke**)

smooch hooch mooch pooch

smooth soothe

smudge budge drudge fudge grudge judge misjudge nudge

smug bug drug dug jug hug lug mug plug pug rug shrug slug snug thug tug

smuggle juggle snuggle struggle

smut (see **but**)

snack (see **sack**)

snake ache bake brake break cake fake flake forsake headache heartache keepsake make mistake opaque quake rake sake shake stake steak take wake

snap cap chap clap dap flap gap handicap lap map mishap nap rap sap scrap slap snap strap tap trap wrap zap

sniff cliff handkerchief if stiff tiff whiff

sniffle piffle riffle whiffle

snivel civil drivel shrivel swivel

snob blob bob cob fob gob hob hobnob job knob lob mob nob rob slob sob swab throb

snow (see **blow**)

snowy Bowie doughy showy

so afro although banjo beau below bestow blow bow buffalo bungalow calico crossbow crow depot doe domino dough embryo escrow Eskimo flow foe forgo fro gazebo gigolo glow go grow heigh-ho ho-ho hobo hoe incognito indigo Joe know long ago low Mexico mistletoe mow no oboe oh outgrow overflow overgrow overthrow owe Pinocchio plateau po-po quo rainbow ratio roe row sew slow snow Soho status quo stow studio though throw tiptoe to-and-fro toe Tokyo tow tremolo undergo undertow vertigo woe yo yo-yo

soap (see **hope**)

sob blob bob cob fob gob hob hobnob job knob lob mob nob rob slob snob swab throb

sober disrober October prober (see *her*)

society anxiety impropriety notoriety piety propriety sobriety variety

sock (see **shock**)

soda coda pagoda

soft aloft loft oft

sold behold blindfold bold centerfold cold fold foothold foretold gold hold household marigold mold old retold scold told uphold withhold

solitaire (see **air**)

solitary (see **scary**)

solitude allude altitude aptitude attitude delude dude feud fortitude gratitude interlude latitude lewd longitude magnitude multitude nud prelude pursued renewed subdued sued 'tude you'd

solo bolo coco gigolo dolo piccolo polo rollo tremolo

solution (see **revolution**)

solve absolve devolve dissolve evolve involve revolve

some (see **scum**)

some album aquarium auditorium become bum burdensome Christendom come cranium crematorium crumb curriculum drum dumb emporium fee-fi-fo-fum glum gum gymnasium hum kettledrum kingdom martyrdom maximum meddlesome medium millennium minimum mum museum numb opium overcome pendulum petroleum platinum plum premium quarrel-some radium random rum sanitarium scum slum strum succumb sum swum tedium thumb Tom Thumb Tweedledum uranium worrisome yum

somebody body embody gaudy lawdy nobody shoddy toddy

son anyone begun bun comparison done everyone fun Galveston gun hon Hun jettison none nun oblivion one outdone outrun overdone overrun phenomenon pun run shotgun shun simpleton skeleton stun sun ton unison venison won

song along belong bong ding-dong gong Hong Kong long ping-pong prong strong throng wrong

soon afternoon baboon balloon bassoon boon buffoon cartoon cocoon coon croon goon harpoon harvest moon honeymoon lagoon lampoon loon maroon monsoon moon noon platoon prune raccoon saloon spittoon swoon tycoon typhoon (see *tune*)

soothe smooth

sorrow borrow morrow sorrow tomorrow

sought (see **thought**)

sound abound around astound background battleground bloodhound bound compound confound downed dumbfound found ground hound impound merry-go-round mound pound profound renowned resound round spellbound surround underground wound

soup coop droop dupe group hoop loop nincompoop poop scoop sloop stoop swoop troop troupe whoop

source coarse course divorce endorse force horse Norse reinforce remorse resource

space ace base bass brace case chase commonplace debase disgrace displace embrace encase erase face grace lace mace misplace pace place race replace steeplechase trace unlace vase

spare (see **air**)

spark aardvark arc ark bark dark embark hark lark mark narc park patriarch remark shark stark

S

sparrow arrow barrow harrow marrow narrow tarot

sparse farce parse

spasm bioplasm chasm enthusiasm plasm sarcasm

spat (see **at**)

speak beak bleak creek eek freak geek leak meek reek seek tweak weak
week

speech beach breach each impeach leech peach preach reach screech
teach

speed agreed breed centipede concede creed deed exceed feed greed
heed inbreed knead lead mislead need precede proceed read
recede reed secede seed stampede succeed Swede tweed weed

spent (see **bent**)

sperm affirm confirm firm germ reaffirm squirm term worm

spider chider cider decider divider glider insider low-rider outsider provide
rider slider wider

spin again aspirin been begin Benjamin Berlin bin chagrin chin Crooklyn
discipline feminine fin 5x10 genuine gin grin heroine in inn kin
mandolin mannequin masculine moccasin origin pin saccharine sh
sin skin spin thick-and-thin thin tin twin violin win within

splash ash balderdash bash brash cash clash crash dash flash gash gnash
rash rehash slash smash stash thrash trash

splendor (see **tender**)

spoil broil coil foil loyal oil recoil royal toil turmoil

spoken broken heartbroken Hoboken jokin' oaken outspoken smokin'
soakin' token

sponge lunge plunge

spook fluke kook

spooky fluky kooky pooky

sport (see **short**)

spot (see **pot**)

spouse blouse douse grouse house louse madhouse mouse outhouse
penthouse slaughterhouse souse

sprang bang boomerang clang dang fang gang-bang hang orangutan ran
sang slang

sprinkle crinkle periwinkle tinkle twinkle wrinkle

spurn (see **learn**)

squabble bobble cobble gobble hobble wobble

squalor bawler brawler call 'er caller choler collar crawler dollar hauler
        mauler scrawler smaller taller

squander condor conned 'er fonder launder ponder wander yonder

square (see **air**)

squeeze (see **ease**)

squish devilish dish fish gibberish impoverish swish wish

stab blab cab crab dab drab fab gab grab jab lab nab scab slab tab

stack (see **sack**)

staff calf carafe epitaph giraffe graph laugh paragraph phonograph
        photograph polygraph riffraff telegraph

stage age cage gage page rampage sage wage

stagger bagger bragger carpet-bagger dagger swagger tagger

stale (see **ale**)

stall all ball bawl brawl call crawl doll drawl fall gall haul install mall maul
        Montreal nightfall overhaul parasol pitfall protocol rainfall scrawl
        shawl small snowfall sprawl tall thrall wall waterfall y'all

stallion battalion Italian medallion rapscallion scallion

stamp amp camp champ clamp cramp damp lamp ramp vamp

stand and band brand canned command contraband demand expand
        fanned grand hand land panned planned reprimand Rio
        Grande sand

stank bank blank clank crank dank drank flank frank gank Hank jank outrank
        plank prank rank sank shank shrank skank spank tank thank yank

stanza bonanza extravaganza

staple maple papal

star A&R are bar bazaar bizarre car caviar cigar czar disbar far guitar jar par
        radar scar spar tar

starch arch march parch

stare (see **air**)

start apart art cart chart counterpart dart depart heart mart part smart
        sweetheart tart upstart

starve carve

static (see **attic**)

stay (see **say**)

steal appeal automobile Bastille Camille conceal deal eel feel genteel he'll
        heal heel ideal kneel meal mobile peel real reel repeal reveal seal
        she'll spiel squeal steel veal we'll wheel zeal

S

stem Bethlehem condemn Eminem gem hem phlegm requiem them
step footstep pep rep
stew (see **do**)
stick (see **pick**)
still bill chill daffodil distill drill fill frill fulfill gill grill hill ill imbecile instill kill
mill nil quill shrill sill skill spill swill thrill till trill until whippoorwill will
windmill windowsill
stink blink brink chink clink drink fink ink kink link mink pink rink shrink sink
slink wink zinc
stir (see **her**)
stirrup chirrup syrup (see *up*)
stoked choked cloaked coked croaked evoked joked poked provoked
revoked smoked soaked stroked
stolen colon rollin' semicolon (see *in*)
stomp comp pomp romp swamp tromp
stone alone atone backbone baritone blown bone chaperone clone
condone cone cornerstone cyclone flown full-blown full-grown
gramophone grindstone groan grown headstone known k-tone loan
lone microphone milestone moan monotone mown overgrown
overthrown own phone postpone prone saxophone sewn shown
telephone thrown tone trombone unknown xylophone zone
stood brotherhood could fatherhood firewood good Hollyhood Hollywood
hood likelihood livelihood misunderstood motherhood neighborhood
should sisterhood understood withstood womanhood wood would
stop chop cop crop drop eavesdrop flop hip-hop hop lollipop mop plop
pop prop raindrop shop swap tip-top whop
store (see **door**)
stork cork fork New York pitchfork pork torque uncork
storm chloroform conform deform form inform norm perform rainstorm
reform snowstorm swarm transform uniform warm
story accusatory allegory category dormitory dory glory gory hunky-dory
laboratory Lori obligatory observatory oratory Peter Lorre quarry
reformatory retaliatory sorry story territory Tory
strange arrange change derange estrange exchange range
strangle angle dangle entangle jangle mangle spangle tangle triangle wrangle
strap cap chap clap dap flap gap handicap lap map mishap nap rap sap
scrap slap snap strap tap trap wrap zap

stream beam cream deem dream esteem extreme gleam ream regime scheme scream seam seen steam supreme team teem

street athlete beat beet bittersweet bleat cheat compete complete conceit concrete deceit defeat delete deplete discreet discrete eat elite feat feet fleet greet heat incomplete indiscreet meat meet mistreat neat obsolete parakeet receipt repeat retreat seat sheet sleet sweat suite treat wheat

strength length

stress (see **confess**)

stricken chicken quicken sicken thicken (see *in*)

strict addict conflict constrict contradict convict derelict evict flicked inflict licked predict pricked

strike bike hike like mike spike tyke

strong along belong bong ding-dong gong Hong Kong long ping-pong prong song throng wrong

stronger longer

struck amuck buck chuck cluck deduct duck horror-struck luck muck pluck potluck puck suck truck tuck

struggle juggle smuggle snuggle

strum (see **scum**)

strung (see **young**)

strut (see **but**)

stud blood bud cud dud flood mud scud spud thud

stuff (see **bluff**)

stuffy fluffy huffy puffy

stump bump chump clump dump hump jump lump plump rump slump thump trump ump

stunk bunk chunk clunk crunk cyberpunk drunk dunk flunk funk hunk junk monk p-funk plunk punk shrunk skunk slunk spunk sunk trunk

stunt affront blunt brunt bunt confront forefront front grunt hunt punt runt shunt

stupid Cupid

style (see **smile**)

stylin' beguilin' complin' defilin' filin' pilin' rilin' smilin'

subject (see **defect**)

subtle cuttle rebuttal scuttle shuttle (see *puddle*)

suburb blurb 'burb curb disturb herb perturb Serb superb verb

S

such clutch crutch Dutch hutch inasmuch much retouch touch

suck amuck buck chuck cluck deduct duck horror-struck luck muck pluck
potluck puck struck truck tuck

sue (see **knew**)

suffer bluffer buffer duffer gruffer puffer rougher tougher

suggestion congestion digestion indigestion ingestion question

suicidal bridal bridle homicidal idle idol tidal

suit (see **shoot**)

suite (see **sweet**)

suitor commuter computer cuter muter neuter persecutor polluter
prosecutor tutor

sulk bulk hulk

summer comer drummer dumber hummer newcomer strummer

sun (see **son**)

sung among clung dung flung high-strung hung lung rung slung sprung
strung stung swung tongue unstrung unsung wrung young

sunk bunk chunk clunk crunk cyberpunk drunk dunk flunk funk hunk junk
monk p-funk plunk punk shrunk skunk slunk spunk stunk trunk

sunny bunny funny honey money

sunrise (see **lies**)

sunset alphabet bayonet bet brunette cabinet cadet cigarette clarinet
cornet corvette debt duet forget fret gazette get jet Joliet Juliet let
luncheonette marionette met net omelet pet quartet regret roulette
set silhouette Somerset sweat threat Tibet toilette upset vet 'vette
violet wet yet

super cooper hooper looper snooper stupor trooper

superb blurb 'burb curb disturb herb perturb Serb suburb verb

superficial artificial beneficial initial judicial official sacrificial

superior exterior inferior interior ulterior

superstition (see **tradition**)

supper upper

supportive (see **abortive**)

sure allure armature assure brochure caricature cocksure cure demure
endure ensure expenditure immature impure insecure insure liqueur
literature lure manicure manure mature miniature obscure overture
pedicure premature pure reassure secure signature tablature
temperature your

S

surf nerf serf turf

surge (see **verge**)

surgeon burgeon emergin' mergin' sturgeon surgin' urgin' virgin

surgery perjury

survival arrival revival rival

suspect (see **defect**)

suspected affected bisected corrected defected deflected detected
directed disaffected dissected effected erected expected infected
inflected inspected intersected neglected objected perfected
protected reflected respected resurrected unaffected unexpected

suspicious (see **vicious**)

swag bag brag do-rag drag flag gag hag lag mag nag rag sag shag slag snag
stag swag tag wag

swagger carpetbagger dagger stagger

swallow Apollo follow hollow wallow

swam (see **am**)

swamp prompt stomp

swan Amazon Babylon begone bonbon Bonn brawn chiffon con Don
dawn drawn fawn gone hexagon John lawn lexicon octagon on
Oregon pawn pentagon silicon undergone upon withdrawn
wanton yawn

swear affair air anywhere aware bare bear billionaire blare care chair
compare dare debonair declare despair disrepair else-where
everywhere fair fare flair flare glare hair hare heir impair legionnaire
mare midair millionaire nightmare pair pare pear Pierre prayer
prepare rare ready-to-wear repair scare snare solitaire somewhere
spare square stair stare tear their there thoroughfare unaware
underwear unfair ware wear where

sweat (see **sunset**)

sweater better cheddar debtor getter letter setter wetter

sweet (see **street**)

sweetly completely concretely discreetly indiscreetly fleetly neatly

sweetie meaty treaty

swept accept adept crept except intercept kept overslept slept
stepped wept

swift drift gift lift shift spendthrift thrift

swig big dig fig gig jig pig rig thingamajig twig underdig wig

swim brim dim Eminem grim gym hymn limb pseudonym skim slim trim whim
swindle dwindle kindle rekindle spindle
swing (see **sing**)
swipe archetype gripe hype pipe prototype ripe stereotype stripe type wipe
swirl curl earl girl hurl pearl twirl whirl
switch bewitch bitch ditch enrich glitch hitch pitch rich snitch stitch
        twitch which
swollen bowlin' rollin' stolen
swamp comp pomp romp stomp tromp
sword aboard accord afford award board bored ford harpsichord hoard lord
        overboard poured reward shuffleboard soared ward
swore (see **door**)
syllable fillable tillable
symbol cymbal nimble thimble

> Rap was territorial. It came from the gang
> wars; I don't know if a lot of people know
> that many of the rappers came from the gang
> wars of the 70s. Some became DJs, MCs; some
> became security. So it melted over into rap
> music, protecting their territory.
>
> —Art Armstrong, early hip-hop promoter
> and Bronx club owner
>
> (Yes, Yes, Y'all: Oral History of
> Hip-Hop's First Decade
> by Jim Fricke, Charlie Ahearn)

t

t (see **be**)

tab blab cab crab dab drab fab gab grab jab lab nab scab slab stab

table (see **able**)

tackle cackle crackle hackle ramshackle shackle

tad (see **mad**)

tag bag brag do-rag drag flag gag hag lag mag nag rag sag shag slag snag stag swag wag

take ache bake brake break cake fake flake forsake headache heartache keepsake make mistake opaque quake rake shake snake stake steak wake

taken achin' bacon fakin' forsaken Jamaican makin' mistaken overtaken shaken undertaken unshaken waken

talk Bangkok beanstalk boondock cock cornstalk clock crock deadlock defrock dock dreadlock flintlock flock frock gawk glock gridlock hawk hock J. S. Bach jock knock Little Rock livestock lock mock Mohawk padlock peacock rock shock sidewalk small Tupac smock sock squawk stalk stock tomahawk unlock walk wok

tall all ball bawl brawl call crawl doll drawl fall gall haul install mall maul Montreal nightfall overhaul parasol pitfall protocol rainfall scrawl shawl small snowfall sprawl stall thrall wall waterfall y'all

tame (see **aim**)

tangle angle dangle entangle jangle mangle spangle strangle triangle wrangle

tango fandango mango

tank bank blank clank crank dank drank flank frank gank Hank jank outrank plank prank rank sank shank shrank skank spank stank thank yank

tap cap chap clap dap flap gap handicap lap map mishap nap rap sap scrap slap snap strap trap wrap zap

tape (see **ape**)

tarnish garnish varnish

task ask bask cask flask mask masque

taste baste aftertaste braced chaste distaste faced freckle-faced haste hatchet-faced lambaste paste waist waste

tattoo (see **do**)

tavern cavern

T

tax ax backs fax jacks lax max relax packs Saks sax slacks wax

taxes axes battle-axes relaxes saxes waxes

tea (see **be**)

teach beach breach each impeach leech peach preach reach
screech speech

teacher bleacher creature feature preacher screecher

team beam cream deem dream esteem extreme gleam ream regime
scheme scream seam seen steam stream supreme teem

tear adhere appear atmosphere auctioneer beer bombardier career cashier
cavalier chandelier cheer clear dear deer disappear ear engineer fear
financier frontier gear hear hemisphere here insincere interfere jeer
lavaliere leer mere mountaineer near overhear overseer peer
persevere pioneer queer racketeer reappear rear revere seer severe
shear sheer sincere smear sneer spear sphere stratosphere veneer
volunteer year

tearful cheerful earful fearful

tease (see **ease**)

tedium medium (see *some*)

teeny Bellini fettuccini genie meany Mussolini scaloppini weenie

teeth beneath heath teeth underneath wreath

tell bell belle Carmel carrousel cell clientele dell dwell excel farewell fell gel
hell hotel infidel knell mademoiselle personnel sell shell smell spell
well yell

temperature (see **pure**)

tempt attempt contempt dreamt exempt unkempt

tempted attempted exempted pre-empted

tender bender blender contender defender extender fender gender lender
mender offender pretender sender slender spender splendor
surrender suspender vendor weekender

tense (see **fence**)

T

tension abstention apprehension ascension attention comprehension
condescension convention dissension detention dimension
dissension extension intention intervention invention mention
retention suspension

term affirm confirm firm germ reaffirm sperm squirm worm

terrific hieroglyphic horrific pacific prolific scientific specific

terror bearer carer darer error wearer

testimony acrimony alimony baloney bony crony macaroni matrimony
      patrimony phony pony sanctimony stony Tony

text context flexed next pretext vexed

thank bank blank clank crank dank drank flank frank gank Hank jank
      outrank plank prank rank sank shank shrank skank spank stank
      tank yank

thankful tankful (see *bull*)

thaw (see **draw**)

theft deft left

them Bethlehem condemn Emenim gem hem phlegm requiem stem

then amen citizen den fen hen hydrogen Ken oxygen pen regimen
      specimen ten yen Zen

theory teary weary (see *be*)

there affair air anywhere aware bare bear billionaire blare care chair
      compare dare debonair declare despair disrepair elsewhere
      everywhere fair fare flair glare hair hare heir impair legionnaire mare
      midair millionaire nightmare pair pare pear Pierre prayer prepare rare
      ready-to-wear repair scare snare solitaire somewhere spare square
      stair stare swear tear their thoroughfare unaware underwear unfair
      ware wear where

thick arithmetic arsenic brick candlestick candlewick Catholic chick click
      copasetic flick heartsick hick kick lick limerick love-sick lunatic
      maverick medic nick pick sick slick stick tic tick wick

thief beef belief brief chief disbelief grief leaf relief

thin (see **been**)

thing (see **sing**)

think blink brink chink clink drink fink ink kink link mink pink rink shrink sink
      slink stink wink zinc

thirst burst cursed first nursed outburst versed worst

this abyss amiss analysis armistice bliss carcass cowardice dis dismiss
      emphasis gangstress hiss hypothesis kiss miss mistress nemesis
      prejudice Swiss synthesis

thorough borough burrow furrow

thought astronaut bought brought caught cosmonaut fought naught ought
      overwrought sought taught wrought

threat (see **sunset**)

thrill bill chill daffodil distill drill fill frill fulfill gill grill hill ill imbecile instill kill
  mill nil quill shrill sill skill spill still swill till trill until whippoorwill will
  windmill windowsill
thriller caterpillar chiller distiller driller filler instiller killer pillar shriller spiller
  swiller tiller
throat afloat antidote bloat boat c-note coat connote denote dote float
  footnote gloat goat misquote moat note oat overcoat promote
  quote remote riverboat rote smote tote turncoat underwrote vote
  wrote throb blob bob cob gob hob hobnob job knob lob mob nob
  rob slob snob sob
throw (see **blow**)
thrown alone atone backbone baritone blown bone chaperone clone
  condone cone cornerstone cyclone flown full-blown full-grown
  gramophone grindstone groan grown headstone known k-tone loan
  lone microphone milestone moan monotone mown overgrown
  overthrown own phone postpone prone saxophone sewn shown
  stone telephone tone trombone unknown xylophone zone
thrust (see **trust**)
thug bug drug dug jug hug lug mug plug pug rug shrug slug smug snug tug
thumb album aquarium auditorium become bum burdensome
  Christendom come cranium crematorium crumb curriculum dumb
  drum emporium fee-fi-fo-fum glum gum gymnasium hum
  kettledrum kingdom martyrdom maximum meddlesome medium
  millennium minimum mum museum numb opium overcome
  pendulum petroleum platinum plum premium quarrelsome radium
  random rum sanitarium scum slum some strum succumb sum
  swum tedium Tom Thumb Tweedledum uranium worrisome yum
thunder blunder plunder under wonder
thus (see **us**)
tick arithmetic arsenic brick candlestick candlewick Catholic chick click
  copasetic flick heartsick hick kick lick limerick love-sick lunatic
  maverick medic nick pick sick slick stick thick tic wick
ticket cricket picket thicket wicked wicket (see *it*)
ticking bricking clicking flicking kicking licking pricking slicking sticking
tide beside bona fide bride collide confide countryside decide defied died
  dignified divide eyed fireside guide hide hillside homicide inside lied
  outside override pride provide reside ride side slide snide stride
  subdivide subside suicide tried wide yuletide

T

tight (see **write**)

tilt built guilt hilt jilt kilt quilt spilt stilt Vanderbilt wilt

time chime climb crime dime I'm lime mime pantomime prime rhyme slime show time summertime thyme

tingle intermingle jingle Kris Kringle mingle shingle single

tint flint hint lint mint peppermint print spearmint splint sprint squint

tip battleship chip clip dip drip equip flip grip gyp hip lip nip quip rip scrip ship slip snip strip trip whip zip

tipsy dipsy gypsy Poughkeepsie

tire (see **fire**)

tissue issue (see *you*)

titanic (see **volcanic**)

title entitle recital vital

tizzy busy dizzy frizzy Lizzie Tin Lizzie rizzi

to (see **do**)

toad (see **road**)

toast boast coast foremost furthermost ghost host innermost most post roast whipping post

together altogether feather Heather leather tether weather whether (see *her*)

toil broil coil foil loyal oil recoil royal spoil turmoil

told behold blindfold bold centerfold cold fold foothold foretold gold hold household marigold mold old retold scold sold uphold withhold

toll (see **roll**)

tomorrow borrow morrow sorrow

ton anyone begun bun comparison done everyone fun Galveston gun hon Hun jettison none nun oblivion one outdone outrun overdone overrun phenomenon pun run shotgun shun simpleton skeleton son stun sun ton unison venison won

tongue (see **young**)

tonic catatonic chronic diatonic enharmonic harmonic ironic monophonic philharmonic phonic platonic polyphonic sonic symphonic

took book brook cook crook hook look mistook nook outlook rook shook undertook

tool April fool cool drool fool ghoul Liverpool overrule pool rule school spool stool whirlpool

tooth booth couth Duluth sleuth truth uncouth youth

torch porch scorch

T

tornado bravado Colorado desperado El Dorado Laredo Mikado

toss across albatross boss cross double-cross floss hoss gloss loss moss
rhinoceros sauce

total anecdotal antidotal

touch clutch crutch Dutch hutch inasmuch much retouch such

touches clutches crutches

tough bluff buff cuff duff enough fluff gruff huff muff powder puff rough
scruff scuff snuff stuff

towel bowel dowel trowel vowel

tower cauliflower cower deflower empower flower horsepower plower
power shower (see *our, her*)

town brown clown crown down downtown drown frown gown hand-me-down
lock-down noun Oaktown renown tumble-down upside down uptown

toy annoy boy convoy corduroy coy decoy destroy employ enjoy homeboy
Illinois joy ploy Roy Savoy soy troy

trace (see **space**)

tracer ace 'er eraser face 'er pacer place 'er (see *her*)

track almanac attack back black Cadillac cardiac clickety-clack crack
egomaniac feedback hack Hackensack haystack jack kleptomaniac
knack lack mack maniac pack plaque Pontiac Prozac quack rack sack
shack slack snack stack tack whack yak zodiac

traction (see **action**)

trade (see **afraid**)

tradition acquisition addition admission ambition ammunition attrition
audition coalition commission competition composition condition
definition demolition deposition disposition edition electrician
emission exhibition expedition exposition extradition fission ignition
imposition inhibition inquisition intermission intuition magician
mathematician mission musician nutrition omission opposition
partition permission petition physician politician position prohibition
proposition recognition rendition repetition requisition statistician
submission superstition technician transmission transposition
transition tuition (see *in*)

tragic magic

trailer inhaler jailer sailor staler wailer whaler

train abstain again airplane arraign ascertain attain brain Cain campaign
cane chain champagne cocaine complain contain crane detain
disdain domain drain entertain explain feign gain grain humane

hurricane hydroplane insane lane main Maine maintain mane migraine obtain ordain pain pane pertain plain plane profane propane rain refrain reign rein remain sane slain Spain sprain stain strain sustain vain vane vein wane windowpane

trait (see **ate**)

trance advance ants chance circumstance dance enhance extravagance finance France glance lance pants prance romance stance

transplant (see **ant**)

trap cap chap clap dap flap gap handicap lap map mishap nap rap sap scrap slap snap strap tap wrap zap

trapeze (see **ease**)

trash ash balderdash bash brash cash clash crash dash flash gash gnash rash rehash slash smash splash stash thrash

traumatic (see **attic**)

travel gavel gravel ravel unravel

treasure displeasure measure pleasure

treat (see **sweet**)

tree (see **be**)

tremendous horrendous stupendous (see *us*)

trench bench clench drench French monkey wrench quench stench wench wrench

trend (see **friend**)

trial denial dial retrial self-denial viol

triangle angle dangle entangle jangle mangle spangle strangle tangle wrangle

tribe bribe circumscribe describe jibe prescribe scribe subscribe vibe

trigger bigger chigger digger rigger rigor swigger tigger vigor

trio Cleo geo Leo Oreo Rio

trip battleship chip clip dip drip equip flip grip gyp hip lip nip quip rip scrip ship slip snip strip tip whip zip

trooper cooper hooper looper snooper stupor super

trot (see **pot**)

troubadour (see **door**)

trouble bubble double rubble stubble

troublemaker (see **acre**)

truce ace-deuce caboose goose juice loose moose noose papoose recluse spruce vamoose

T

truck amuck buck chuck cluck deduct duck horror-struck luck muck pluck potluck puck struck suck tuck

trucker bucker chucker clucker pucker sapsucker seersucker sucker (see *her*)

true (see **do**)

truest bluest newest

truly coolie coolly duly newly ruly unduly unruly

trump bump chump clump dump hump jump lump plump rump slump stump thump ump

trumpet bump it crumpet dump it lump it strumpet thump it

trunk bunk chunk clunk crunk cyberpunk drunk dunk flunk funk hunk junk monk p-funk plunk punk shrunk skunk slunk spunk stunk sunk

trust adjust August bust crust dust disgust distrust encrust entrust gust just lust mistrust must robust rust thrust unjust

truth booth couth Duluth sleuth tooth uncouth youth

try alibi amplify banzai barfly butterfly buy by bye certify clarify crucify cry defy deify deny die dignify diversify dragonfly drive-by dry dye eye firefly fly fry FYI glorify gratify guy high horrify I identify imply July justify lie lullaby modify my mystify notify passerby pie pry qualify rely rye satisfy sci-fi shy sigh signify simplify sky sly specify spry spy terrify testify thigh tie underlie verify why

tub Beelzebub bub club cub grub hub hubbub pub rub rub-a-dub-dub scrub shrub snub stub sub

tube boob cube rube

tug bug drug dug jug hug lug mug plug pug rug shrug slug smug snug thug

tuition (see **tradition**)

tulip julep

tumor bloomer boomer consumer humor rumor

tune attune commune dune immune impugn inopportune June (see *moon*)

tunnel funnel

Tupoc (see **talk**)

turf nerf serf surf

turkey Albuquerque murky perky quirky

turmoil broil coil foil loyal oil recoil royal spoil toil

turn adjourn burn churn concern discern earn fern intern kern learn overturn return sojourn spurn stern taciturn urn yearn

twice advice concise device dice entice ice lice mice nice paradise precise price rice sacrifice spice splice thrice vice

twilight highlight skylight (see *light*)

twin (see **been**)

twinkle crinkle periwinkle sprinkle tinkle wrinkle

twerp burp chirp usurp Wyatt Earp

twist (see **mist**)

twisted assisted enlisted existed fisted insisted listed misted persisted resisted subsisted

twister assister blister mister resister sister (see *her*)

type archetype gripe hype pipe prototype ripe stereotype stripe swipe wipe

tyrant aspirant

Hip-hop is a culture, a way of life, it's a state of mind. It's an urban feeling. It's about where you come from, the streets and being proud of your environment.

—Salt of Salt-N-Pepa

T

u

udder rudder shudder

ugly smugly snugly

ulcer (see *her*)

ultimate befit bit fit 'git grit kit knit hit it jit legit lit mitt nit-wit pit quit sit twit unfit wit zit

umbrella Béla fella' Stella

ump bump chump clump dump hump jump lump plump rump slump stump thump trump

under blunder plunder thunder wonder

underdig big dig fig gig jig pig renege rig swig thingamajig twig wit

underdog analog bog catalog clog cog dog fog demagogue dialogue epilogue flog frog grog hog jog log monologue synagogue travelogue

undercover cover discover hover lover recover rediscover shover (see *her*)

understood brotherhood could fatherhood firewood good Hollyhood Hollywood hood likelihood livelihood misunderstood motherhood neighborhood should sisterhood stood understood withstood womanhood wood would

unicorn adorn airborne born Cape Horn Capricorn corn forlorn horn lovelorn Matterhorn morn mourn popcorn scorn sea borne stillborn sworn warn worn

uniform chloroform conform deform form inform norm perform rainstorm reform snowstorm storm swarm transform warm

union communion disunion reunion

unite blight cite delight excite ignite incite indict invite knight light recite requite reunite right sight spite

universal rehearsal reversal

universe adverse converse curse disburse disperse diverse hearse immerse intersperse inverse nurse purse rehearse reverse terse transverse traverse verse worse

until bill chill daffodil distill drill fill frill fulfill gill grill hill ill imbecile instill kill mill nil quill shrill sill skill spill still swill thrill till trill whippoorwill will windmill windowsill

up buttercup cup fed up hard-up pick-up pup sup

U

upon Amazon Babylon begone bonbon Bonn brawn chiffon con Don dawn
drawn fawn gone hexagon John lawn lexicon octagon on Oregon
pawn pentagon silicon undergone withdrawn wanton yawn

uproot (see **shoot**)

upset alphabet bayonet bet brunette cabinet cadet cigarette clarinet cornet
corvette debt duet forget fret gazette get jet Joliet Juliet let
luncheonette marionette met net omelet pet quartet regret roulette
set silhouette Somerset sunset sweat threat Tibet toilette vet 'vette
violet wet yet

urge converge dirge diverge emerge merge purge scourge serge splurge
submerge surge verge

urgent detergent divergent emergent resurgent

urn (see **learn**)

us   *one syllable:*
bus cuss Gus muss plus pus truss thus
two syllables:
discuss
three syllables:
amorous barbarous blasphemous boisterous cancerous cankerous
cavernous chivalrous courteous curious devious dubious envious
hideous industrious infamous lecherous ludicrous marvelous
murderous nauseous nautilus nebulous numerous octopus ominous
omnibus perilous poisonous ponderous precarious prosperous
ravenous rebellious rigorous riotous scandalous scrupulous sensuous
curious devious dubious envious hideous industrious infamous
lecherous ludicrous marvelous murderous nauseous nautilus
nebulous numerous octopus ominous omnibus perilous poisonous
ponderous precarious prosperous ravenous rebellious rigorous
riotous scandalous scrupulous sensuous serious slanderous stimulus
strenuous studious tedious tempestuous thunderous tortuous
treacherous treasonous various villainous
four or more syllables:
adventurous ambiguous androgynous anonymous conspicuous
contemptuous continuous dangerous delirious erroneous extraneous
famous frivolous furious fuss generous gregarious glorious gratuitous
harmonious hazardous hilarious illustrious incredulous luxurious
miscellaneous monogamous monotonous mysterious notorious oblivious
populous posthumous preposterous presumptuous promiscuous
simultaneous spontaneous tumultuous uproarious victorious

U

use abuse accuse confuse cues deduce diffuse disuse duce excuse induce
     infuse introduce juice misuse obtuse peruse produce profuse reduce
     refuse reproduce seduce Syracuse
user abuse accuser boozer bruiser cruiser lose 'er loser muser oozer refuse
     'er refuser snoozer
utter butter clutter cutter flutter gutter mutter putter shutter sputter
     strutter stutter
Uzi boozy doosy Jacuzzi Susy woosy

"

God bless my enemies. I can't really focus
on what they doing. Why is my life the
focus of your life? Why is my life the
answer to your life? As you see I don't
really pay attention to them. I try to do
my thing. I don't make records about them
or make any comments. It's just them
constantly tagging me, making references
to me, trying to pull me out of my mode.
I'm a peaceful, positive role model making
records. What they try to do is take me
down the back roads of where I used to
be. Let's keep it real, ya keep doing
what you're doing and I'll keep doing
what I'm doing.

"

—Snoop Dogg

U

V

vacate (see **ate**)

vague plague

vain abstain again airplane arraign ascertain attain brain Cain campaign cane chain champagne cocaine complain contain crane detain disdain domain drain entertain explain feign gain grain humane hurricane hydroplane insane lane main Maine maintain mane migraine obtain ordain pain pane pertain plain plane profane propane rain refrain reign rein remain sane slain Spain sprain stain strain sustain train vane vein wane windowpane

valid ballad invalid salad

valley alley dilly-dally rally Sally tally

vamp amp camp champ clamp cramp damp lamp ramp stamp

vandal candle dandle handle sandal scandal

vanilla gorilla guerrilla Manila Priscilla villa

vapors capers rapers scrapers shapers skyscrapers papers (see *her*)

variety anxiety impropriety notoriety piety propriety sobriety society (see **be**)

various (see **us**)

vary carry hare Kari marry miscarry parry (see *cherry*)

vase ace base bass brace case chase commonplace debase disgrace displace embrace encase erase face grace lace mace misplace pace place race replace space steeplechase trace unlace

vast aghast blast cast classed contrast fast flabbergast forecast gassed last mast outlast overcast passed past

vat (see **at**)

vault assault cobalt exalt fault halt malt salt somersault

veejay array bay betray blue jay bouquet bray clay day decay delay disarray dismay display Dr. Dre eh? essay exposé fray gay gray hay hey holiday hooray José Kay lay matinee may moiré naysay negligée obey parlay pay play portray protégé ray résumé ricochet risqué rosé say slay sleigh soufflé stay stray sway they toupee way weigh wordspray x-ray

vegetarian Aquarian Aryan barbarian buryin' Cesarean disciplinarian ferryin' humanitarian libertarian librarian Marion marryin' Rastafarian Sagittarian Unitarian veterinarian

veil (see **ale**)

V

vendor (see **tender**)

vent (see **bent**)

venture adventure denture indenture misadventure

verb blurb 'burb curb disturb herb perturb Serb suburb superb

verbal gerbil herbal

verbose adios bellicose close comatose diagnose dose engross grandiose gross morose nose overdose varicose

verge converge dirge diverge emerge merge purge scourge serge splurge submerge surge urge

vermin determine German merman sermon

verse adverse converse curse disburse disperse diverse hearse immerse intersperse inverse nurse purse rehearse reverse terse transverse traverse universe worse

vessel nestle trestle wrestle

vest arrest attest best blessed breast Bucharest Budapest chest congest contest crest detest digest divest dressed guessed guest infest ingest interest invest jest manifest messed molest nest pest protest request rest second-best suggest test unrest zest

veto bonito mosquito neat-o

vexed context flexed next pretext text

viaduct abduct conduct construct deduct instruct obstruct plucked viaduct

vibe bribe circumscribe describe jibe prescribe scribe subscribe tribe

vice advice concise device dice entice ice lice mice nice paradise precise price rice sacrifice spice splice suffice thrice twice

vicked clicked flicked kicked licked nicked picked slicked ticked wick

vicious ambitious auspicious capricious delicious expeditious factious fictitious judicious malicious nutritious propitious seditious superstitious suspicious

victory (see **be**)

view adieu anew avenue barbecue bayou chew cue curfew debut dew due ensue ewe few guru honeydew hue I.O.U. imbue ingénue interview Jew knew lieu new Nehru overdue pee-ewe pew preview pursue renew residue revenue review spew subdue sue undue yew you (see *do*)

vigor bigger chigger digger rigger rigor swigger tigger trigger

vile aisle awhile beguile bile compile crocodile defile file isle juvenile meanwhile mile Nile pile rile smile style tile while wile worthwhile

V

village pillage tillage
villain billin' chillin' Dylan fillin' illin' willin' (see *in*)
vindictive (see **native**)
vine (see **fine**)
violate (see **ate**)
violence (see **fence**)
viper bagpiper pied piper riper sniper striper swiper typer wiper
virgin burgeon emergin' mergin' sturgeon surgeon surgin' urgin'
virginity (see **be**)
visible divisible indivisible invisible
vision collision decision derision division incision indecision precision
        provision revision supervision television
vital entitle recital title
vivid livid
vocal focal local yokel
vogue brogue rogue
voice choice invoice rejoice
void avoid alkaloid asteroid joyed Lloyd Sigmund Freud tabloid toyed
volcanic Hispanic manic mechanic monomaniac oceanic organic panic
        satanic titanic (see *romantic*)
volley collie dolly finale folly golly jolly melancholy Molly Polly tamale trolley
voodoo (see **do**)
vote afloat antidote bloat boat c-note coat connote denote dote float
        footnote gloat goat misquote moat note oat overcoat promote quote
        remote riverboat rote smote throat tote turncoat underwrote wrote
vouch couch crouch grouch ouch pouch slouch
vow allow avow bough bow brow chow cow disavow endow frau how
        kowtow now ow plough plow row slough somehow sow thou wow
vowel bowel dowel towel trowel
vulture agriculture culture

V

W

whack back almanac attack black Cadillac cardiac clickety-clack egomaniac
feedback hack Hackensack haystack jack kleptomaniac knack lack
mack maniac pack plaque Pontiac Prozac quack rack sack shack slack
snack stack tack track yak zodiac

wag bag brag do-rag drag flag gag hag lag mag nag rag sag shag slag snag
stag swag tag

wage age cage gage page rampage sage stage

waif safe

wait (see **ate**)

wake ache bake brake break cake fake flake forsake headache heartache
keepsake make mistake opaque quake rake shake snake stake steak
take

walk Bangkok beanstalk boondock cock cornstalk clock crock deadlock
defrock dock dreadlock flintlock flock frock gawk glock gridlock hawk
hock J. S. Bach jock knock Little Rock livestock lock mock Mohawk
padlock peacock rock shock sidewalk small talk Tupoc smock sock
squawk stalk stock talk tomahawk unlock wok

wall all ball bawl brawl call crawl doll drawl fall gall haul install mall maul
Montreal nightfall overhaul parasol pitfall protocol rainfall scrawl
shawl small snowfall sprawl stall tall thrall waterfall y'all

wallow Apollo follow hollow swallow

wand beyond blond bond correspond fond dawned pond respond
spawned vagabond yawned

wander condor conned 'er fonder launder ponder squander yonder

want daunt flaunt gaunt haunt jaunt taunt

ward (see **lord**)

warm chloroform conform deform form inform norm perform rainstorm
reform snowstorm storm swarm transform uniform

wart abort assort comfort contort court deport distort escort exhort export
extort fort import passport port quart report resort retort short snort
sort sport support thwart tort transport (see **art**)

wary adversary airy arbitrary beneficiary berry bury canary capillary
cautionary cherry commentary culinary customary dairy
dictionary dietary dignitary disciplinary discretionary evolutionary
extraordinary fairy February ferry functionary hairy hereditary
honorary imaginary incendiary intermediary January Jerry

legendary legionary literary luminary Mary mercenary military momentary monetary mortuary nary necessary obituary ordinary Perry planetary prairie proprietary pulmonary reactionary revolutionary sanctuary sanitary scary secretary seminary sherry solitary stationary temporary Terry very visionary vocabulary voluntary

was abuzz buzz cause coz does fuzz

was applause because cause clause claws gauze laws menopause Oz pause paws Santa Claus

wash awash frosh galosh gosh hogwash josh Macintosh posh quash slosh squash swash

waste baste aftertaste braced chaste distaste faced freckle-faced haste hatchet-faced lambaste paste taste two-faced waist

watch blotch botch crotch debauch hopscotch notch Scotch wristwatch

water blotter daughter hotter otter plotter slaughter spotter squatter trotter

wave behave brave cave concave crave engrave forgave gave grave knave pave rave save shave slave waive

wax ax backs fax jacks lax max relax packs Saks sax slacks tax

way array bay betray blue jay bouquet bray clay day decay delay disarray dismay display Dr. Dre eh? essay exposé fray gay gray hay hey holiday hooray José Kay lay matinee may moiré naysay negligée obey parlay pay play portray protégé ray résumé ricochet risqué rosé say slay sleigh soufflé stay stray sway they toupee veejay weigh wordspray x-ray

we (see **be**)

wealth commonwealth health stealth

weary bleary cheery deary dreary eerie Erie leery query teary

weasel diesel easel measles

weather altogether feather Heather leather tether together whether (see *her*)

weave achieve believe bereave conceive disbelieve eve grieve heave leave perceive receive relieve reprieve retrieve sleeve

web deb ebb

wed ahead bed bedspread bread bred coed dead dread fed figurehead fled flowerbed fountainhead gingerbread head inbred lead led misled misread overfed read red riverbed said shed shred sled sped spread thoroughbred thread underfed unthread

wedge allege dredge edge fledge hedge ledge privilege sacrilege sledge

weed agreed breed centipede concede creed deed exceed feed greed
heed inbreed knead lead mislead need precede proceed read
recede reed secede seed speed stampede succeed Swede tweed

weep barkeep cheep creep deep heap keep leap peep reap seep sheep
sleep steep sweep

weight (see **ate**)

weird appeared beard cleared disappeared feared jeered neared
persevered smeared speared

welch belch squelch

weld felled held meld upheld

well bell belle Carmel carrousel cell clientele dell dwell excel farewell fell
gel hell hotel infidel knell mademoiselle personnel sell shell smell
spell tell yell

welt belt Celt dealt felt heartfelt melt pelt

went (see **bent**)

wept accept adept crept except intercept kept overslept slept stepped swept

were amateur blur chauffeur concur confer connoisseur defer demur deter
fur her gansta incur infer inter myrrh occur per prefer purr recur sir
slur spur stir transfer voyageur whir

wet alphabet bayonet bet brunette cabinet cadet cigarette clarinet cornet
corvette debt duet epithet etiquette forget fret gazette get jet Joliet
Juliet let luncheonette marionette net omelet pet quartet regret
roulette set silhouette Somerset sunset sweat threat Tibet toilette
upset vet 'vette violet yet

wharf dwarf

what (see *but, hot*)

wheat (see **sweet**)

wheel appeal automobile Bastille Camille conceal deal eel feel genteel he'll
heal heel ideal kneel meal mobile peel real reel repeal reveal seal
she'll spiel squeal steal steel veal we'll zeal

where affair air anywhere aware bare bear billionaire blare care chair
compare dare debonair declare despair disrepair elsewhere
everywhere fair fare flair glare hair hare heir impair legionnaire mare
midair millionaire nightmare pair pare pear Pierre prayer prepare rare
ready-to-wear repair scare snare solitaire somewhere spare square
stair stare swear tear their there thoroughfare unaware underwear
unfair ware wear

which bewitch bitch ditch enrich glitch hitch pitch rich snitch stitch switch twitch

whiff cliff handkerchief if sniff stiff tiff

while aisle awhile beguile bile compile crocodile defile file isle juvenile meanwhile mile Nile pile rile smile style tile vile wile worthwhile

whim brim dim Eminem grim gym hymn limb pseudonym skim slim swim trim

whimper scrimper shrimper skimper

whip battleship chip clip dip drip equip flip grip gyp hip lip nip quip rip scrip ship slip snip strip tip trip zip

whirl curl earl girl hurl pearl swirl twirl

whisker brisker frisker risker

whiskey frisky risky

whisper crisper (see *her*)

whistle bristle dismissal gristle missal missile sisal thistle

white (see **fight**)

whiz biz fizz frizz his is quiz showbiz 'tis

whole bowl buttonhole cajole casserole coal control dole droll enroll goal hole loophole Maypole mole Old King Cole oriole parole patrol pole poll porthole role roll scroll tadpole toll troll

whom bloom boom broom cloakroom doom entomb flume gloom groom room tomb womb zoom

whopper (see **proper**)

whore (see **door**)

whose blues booze bruise choose cruise lose news ooze shoes snooze

why alibi amplify banzai barfly butterfly buy by bye certify clarify crucify cry defy deify deny die dignify diversify dragonfly drive-by dry dye eye firefly fly fry FYI glorify gratify guy high horrify I identify imply July justify lie lullaby modify my mystify notify passerby pie pry qualify rely rye satisfy sci-fi shy sigh signify simplify sky sly specify spry spy terrify testify thigh tie try underlie verify

wick arithmetic arsenic brick candlestick candlewick Catholic chick click copasetic flick heartsick hick kick lick limerick love-sick lunatic maverick medic music nick pick sick slick stick thick tic tick

wicked cricket picket thicket ticket wicket (see *it*)

wide beside bona fide bride collide confide countryside decide defied died dignified divide eyed fireside guide hide hillside homicide inside lied outside override pride provide reside ride side slide snide stride subdivide subside suicide tide tried yuletide

wider chider cider decider divider glider insider low-rider outsider provider rider slider spider

wield battlefield Chesterfield field shield yield

wife afterlife jackknife knife life strive wife

wig big dig fig gig jig pig renege rig swig thingamajig twig underdig

wiggle giggle jiggle squiggle wriggle

wild child dialed mild piled smiled

will bill chill daffodil distill drill frill fulfill gill grill hill ill imbecile instill kill mill nil quill shrill sill skill spill still swill thrill till trill until whippoorwill will windmill windowsill

willing billing chilling distilling drilling filling fulfilling instilling killing milling shrilling spilling stilling swilling thrilling tilling unwilling

willow armadillo billow peccadillo pillow

wilt built guilt hilt jilt kilt quilt spilt stilt tilt Vanderbilt

wimp blimp gimp imp limp pimp shrimp skimp

win again aspirin been begin Benjamin Berlin bin chagrin chin Crooklyn discipline feminine fin 5x10 genuine gin grin heroine in inn kin mandolin mannequin masculine moccasin origin pin saccharine shin sin skin spin thick-and-thin thin tin twin violin within

wind behind bind blind find grind hind humankind kind mastermind mind remind signed unkind unwind wined

wind disciplined grinned rescind sinned (see *bend*)

wine (see *fine*)

wing anything bring cling ding evening everything fling king ring sing sling spring sting string swing thing wring (add "-ing" to action words, e.g., run[ning], etc.)

wink blink brink chink clink drink fink ink kink link mink pink rink shrink sink slink stink zinc

winner B. F. Skinner beginner breadwinner dinner inner sinner skinner spinner thinner

wino albino rhino (see *know*)

winter hinter printer splinter sprinter squinter tinter (see *her*)

wipe archetype gripe hype pipe prototype ripe stereotype stripe swipe type

wiping griping piping stereotyping striping swiping typing

wire acquire admire amplifier aspire attire buyer choir conspire crier cryer desire dire drier dryer entire esquire expire fire flier friar higher hire inquire inspire justifier liar magnifier multiplier mystifier perspire prior prophesier require retire satisfier sire squire supplier testifier tire transpire

wise (see **lies**)

wiser advertiser adviser agonizer analyzer apologizer equalizer eulogizer exerciser fertilizer geyser harmonizer idolizer miser riser sizer surpriser

wish devilish dish fish gibberish impoverish squish swish

wisp crisp lisp

wit befit bit fit 'git grit kit knit hit it jit legit lit nit-wit pit quit sit twit unfit zit

witchcraft craft draft draught graft overdraft

witches bitches ditches enriches hitches itches niches pitches riches stitches switches twitches

witty city committee ditty gritty kitty pity pretty self-pity

wizard gizzard lizard scissored

woe (see **blow**)

woes arose chose close compose decompose depose disclose dispose doze enclose expose foreclose froze goes hose impose indispose knows nose owes pose predispose presuppose prose rose suppose those toes transpose

woke artichoke baroque bloke broke choke cloak coke croak evoke folk invoke joke oak poke provoke revoke smoke soak spoke stroke toke yoke

womb bloom boom broom cloakroom doom entomb flume gloom groom room tomb whom zoom

wonder blunder plunder under thunder

wool bull cock-and-bull do-able full marble pull (see *beautiful*)

word absurd bird blackbird bluebird curd heard herd Kurd hummingbird ladybird mockingbird overheard third yellowbird

wordsmith accompanist analyst anarchist anthropologist archeologist assist biologist Calvinist capitalist coexist communist consist cyst desist dismissed egoist essayist evangelist exist exorcist fatalist gist hissed humanist humorist idealist imperialist insist journalist kissed list lobbyist Methodist missed mist moralist motorist nationalist novelist organist perfectionist pharmacist pianist plagiarist psychologist romanticist satirist sentimentalist

W

socialist soloist specialist strategist terrorist theologist theorist twist ventriloquist vocalist wrist

wordspray (see **x-ray**)

work clerk handiwork irk jerk Kirk lurk murk overwork perk quirk shirk s mirk Turk

worker book 'er hook 'er lurker shirker shook 'er smirker snooker took 'er (see *her*)

world underworld

worm affirm confirm firm germ reaffirm sperm squirm term

worn adorn airborne born Cape Horn Capricorn corn forlorn horn lovelorn Matterhorn morn mourn popcorn scorn sea borne stillborn sworn unicorn warn

worry curry flurry fury hurry jury Missouri scurry slurry surrey

worse adverse converse curse disburse disperse diverse hearse immerse intersperse inverse nurse purse rehearse reverse terse transverse traverse universe verse

worst burst cursed first nursed outburst thirst versed

worth birth dearth earth girth mirth

would brotherhood could fatherhood firewood good Hollyhood Hollywood hood likelihood livelihood misunderstood motherhood neighborhood should sisterhood stood understood withstood womanhood wood

wound (see **sound**)

woven Beethoven cloven interwoven

wow allow avow bough bow brow chow cow disavow endow frau how kowtow now ow plough plow row slough somehow sow thou vow

wrap cap chap clap dap flap gap handicap lap map mishap nap rap sap scrap slap snap strap tap trap zap

wrapper capper clapper dapper flapper handicapper rapper slapper snapper tapper whippersnapper wiretapper yapper

wrath aftermath bath homeopath math path psychopath sociopath

wreck check Czech deck fleck heck neck peck project Quebec speck trek

wrecker checker chequer decker double-decker exchequer pecker woodpecker

wrench bench clench drench French monkey wrench quench stench trench wench

wrestle nestle trestle vessel

wretch catch etch fetch kvetch retch sketch stretch wretch

H

wring (see **sing**)

wrinkle crinkle periwinkle sprinkle tinkle twinkle

wrist (see **mist**)

write appetite bite blight bright byte contrite copyright daylight delight despite dynamite excite Fahrenheit fight flight fright headlight height ignite invite kite knight light midnight might moonlight night outright parasite plight polite quite recite reunite right satellite sight site sleight slight spite starlight sunlight tight trite twilight unite white

written bitten Britain Briton kitten mitten smitten (see *in*)

wrong along belong bong ding-dong gong Hong Kong long ping-pong prong song strong throng

wrote afloat antidote bloat boat c-note coat connote denote dote float footnote gloat goat misquote moat note oat overcoat promote quote remote riverboat rote smote throat tote turncoat underwrote vote

wrought (see **thought**)

X

x-rated (see **hated**)

x-ray array away bay betray blue jay bouquet bray clay day decay delay disarray dismay display Dr. Dre eh? essay exposé fray gay gray hay hey holiday hooray José Kay lay matinee may moiré naysay negligée obey parlay pay play portray protégé ray résumé ricochet risqué rosé say slay sleigh soufflé say stay stray sway they toupee way weigh wordspray

Xerox box chickenpox e-box equinox fox mailbox orthodox ox paradox rocks socks stocks

xylophone (see **alone**)

> Hip-Hop at its root is the reflection of
> a lost people still trying to find
> themselves.
>
> —Chuck D of Public Enemy

X

Y

yacht apricot blot Camelot clot cot cybot dot forget-me-not forgot fought gavotte got hot hot-shot jot knot lot not plot pot robot rot shot slingshot somewhat spot squat swat tot trot watt what

yank bank blank clank crank dank drank flank frank gank Hank jank outrank plank prank rank sank shank shrank skank spank stank tank thank

Yankee cranky hanky hanky-panky lanky scanky

yard avant-garde bogard card chard discard disregard guard hard lard regard retard tarred

yarn barn darn

yawn Amazon Babylon begone bonbon Bonn brawn chiffon con Don dawn drawn fawn gone hexagon John lawn lexicon octagon on Oregon pawn pentagon silicon undergone upon withdrawn wanton

year adhere appear atmosphere auctioneer beer bombardier career cashier cavalier chandelier cheer clear dear deer disappear ear engineer fear financier frontier gear hear hemisphere here insincere interfere jeer lavaliere leer mere mountaineer near overhear overseer peer persevere pioneer queer racketeer reappear rear revere seer severe shear sheer sincere smear sneer spear sphere stratosphere tear veneer volunteer

yearn adjourn burn churn concern discern earn fern intern kern learn overturn return sojourn spurn stern taciturn turn urn

yell bell belle Carmel carrousel cell clientele dell dwell excel farewell fell gel hell hotel infidel knell mademoiselle personnel sell shell smell spell tell well

yellow bellow cello delo fellow hello Jell-O mellow Othello

yelp help kelp

yes access address baroness bashfulness bitterness bless caress chess cleverness cloudiness compress confess craziness deadliness depress digress distress dizziness dress duress eagerness easiness eeriness emptiness excess express finesse foolish-ness guess happiness haziness homelessness idleness impress joyfulness laziness less limitless Loch Ness lustfulness mess nervousness obsess openness oppress outrageousness penniless playfulness possess press progress queasiness recess regress repossess repress rockiness seediness shallowness silkiness sleaziness sleepiness sneakiness SOS spaciousness spitefulness stress success suppress thoughtfulness transgress uselessness viciousness willingness worldliness youthfulness

yet alphabet bayonet bet brunette cabinet cadet cigarette clarinet cornet corvette debt duet epithet etiquette forget fret gazette get jet Joliet Juliet let luncheonette marionette net omelet pet quartet regret roulette set silhouette Somerset sunset sweat threat Tibet toilette upset vet 'vette violet wet

yield battlefield Chesterfield field shield wield

yodel modal nodal

yoga Saratoga toga

yogurt (see **shirt**)

yoke (see **joke**)

yonder condor conned 'er fonder launder ponder squander wander

you adieu anew avenue barbecue bayou chew cue curfew debut dew due ensue ewe few guru honeydew hue I.O.U. imbue ingénue interview Jew knew lieu new Nehru overdue pee-ewe pew preview pursue renew residue revenue review spew subdue sue undue view yew (see *do*)

young among clung dung flung high-strung hung lung rung slung sprung strung stung sung swung tongue unstrung unsung wrung

your (see **door**)

your allure armature assure brochure caricature cocksure cure demure endure ensure expenditure immature impure insecure insure liqueur literature lure manicure manure mature miniature obscure overture pedicure premature pure reassure secure signature sure tablature temperature

yourself elf herself himself itself myself self shelf

youth booth couth Duluth sleuth tooth truth uncouth

yum album aquarium auditorium become bum burdensome Christendom come cranium crematorium crumb curriculum drum dump emporium fee-fi-fo-fum glum gum gymnasium hum kettledrum kingdom martyrdom maximum meddlesome medium millennium minimum mum museum numb opium overcome pendulum petroleum platinum plum premium quarrel-some radium random rum sanitarium scum slum some strum succumb sum swum tedium thumb Tom Thumb Tweedledum uranium worrisome yum

yuppie guppy puppy

Z

zap cap chap clap dap flap gap handicap lap map mishap nap rap sap
scrap slap snap strap tap trap wrap

zeal (see **wheel**)

zealous jealous sell us tell us (see *us*)

zebra abc-ya duh Oprah extra (see *raw*)

Zen amen citizen den fen hen hydrogen Ken oxygen pen regimen
specimen ten then yen

zinc blink brink chink clink drink fink ink kink link mink pink rink shrink sink
slink stink think wink

zine bean between caffeine canteen chlorine clean codeine Colleen
convene cuisine dean demean evergreen foreseen gasoline Gene
green guillotine Halloween in-between intervene kerosene lean lien
machine marine mean Nazarene nectarine nicotine obscene preen
quarantine queen ravine routine sardine scene seen serene spleen
submarine tambourine tangerine teen thirteen (etc.) Vaseline
velveteen wintergreen wolverine

zip battleship chip clip dip drip equip flip grip gyp hip lip nip quip rip scrip
ship slip snip strip tip trip whip

zit befit bit fit 'git grit kit knit hit it jit legit lit mitt nit-wit pit quit sit twit unfit
ultimate wit zit

zodiac (see **track**)

zone alone atone backbone baritone blown bone chaperone clone
condone cone cornerstone cyclone flown full-blown full-grown
gramophone grindstone groan grown headstone known k-tone loan
lone microphone milestone moan monotone mown overgrown
overthrown own phone postpone prone saxophone sewn shown
stone telephone thrown tone trombone unknown xylophone zone

zoo accrue ado bamboo blew blue boo boohoo brew caribou cashew clue
construe coo coup crew cuckoo do drew flew flue glue gnu goo grew
Hindu hitherto hullabaloo igloo impromptu into issue Kalamazoo
kangaroo kazoo Kickapoo misconstrue moo outdo overdo overthrew
peek-a-boo Peru poo rendezvous screw shampoo shoe shoo shrew Sioux
slew slue stew taboo tattoo threw through tissue to too true two undo
voodoo wahoo well-to-do who withdrew woo yahoo zoo Zulu (see **you**)

zoom bloom boom broom cloakroom doom entomb flume gloom groom
room tomb whom womb